The Macroeconomics of the Executive Power Branch

The Macroeconomics of the Executive Power Branch

S.S. Khrystenko

iUniverse, Inc.
New York Lincoln Shanghai

The Macroeconomics of the Executive Power Branch

iUniverse books may be ordered through booksellers or by contacting:

iUniverse
2021 Pine Lake Road, Suite 100
Lincoln, NE 68512
www.iuniverse.com
1-800-Authors (1-800-288-4677)

ISBN-13: 978-0-595-41959-3 (pbk)
ISBN-13: 978-0-595-86299-3 (ebk)
ISBN-10: 0-595-41959-3 (pbk)
ISBN-10: 0-595-86299-3 (ebk)

Printed in the United States of America

Contents

Introduction

Today, in the economic theory, there are no chapters in which the structure of the expenses and result of the executive power branch is examined.

Today, the people have a specific view on the services of the executive power branch should be taken into account in the results of not only receipts from the taxes, police services, military services.

But the executive power creates much more services. It finances educational branches, enlightenment, the first national television and the first radio channel, public transport, medicine and the military.

The services of these branches, financed from the budget, should be taken into account in the accounting department of the executive branch of authority, but not only in the section of expenses, but also in the section of results.[1]

Problems of new calculations of resources executive branch of power author considers in the books:

Vol. 1 The Economics: Enlightenment and Entertainment
Vol. 2 The Macroeconomy of the Education Sphere
Vol. 3 The Macroeconomy of the Mass Media Sphere
Vol. 4 The Macroeconomy of the Transport Sphere
Vol. 5 The Macroeconomy of the Military Sphere

---

1 The marked rule is first economic axiom of the executive branch of authority.

CHAPTER 1

THE THREE BRANCHES OF THE STATE POWER

Two thousand years ago, the Romans proposed a state system comprising the legislative, executive and judicial branches of power, a model of statehood widely applied now in democratic countries. It is essential that the quality of economic space of a state is dependent upon the services of these three branches of power.

I suggest that the services of the three branches of power should be arranged in a three-dimensional space in the following way:

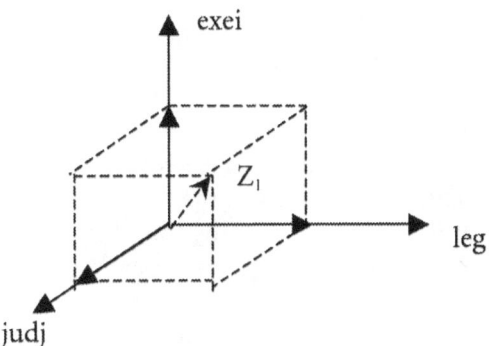

, where
-on axis X—single service vector of the legislative power (leg);
-on axis Y—single service vector of the executive power (exei);
-on axis Z—single service vector of the judicial power (judj).

The above services are being reproduced every hour, every day, every year.
The complex vector R of the three types of services can be recorded as follows:

$$R = \pm \text{«leg»} \pm \text{«exe»} i \pm \text{«jud»} j$$

where

i, j—imaginary units reflecting versatile character of power services.

If the services of the three branches of power are not examined in a three dimensional space, the services of a separate branch of power overlap the services of the other branches and so forth.

This way of examination makes it difficult to comprehend what is going on in the state power sphere. The arrangement of the power vectors in the Cartesian three-dimensional system of coordinates may be considered as rewarding finding on the way of cognizing the economy of state power.

Each branch of power offers its own specific subject of labor as well as particular expenses and results.

Today, in the economic theory, some chapters are missing sections concerning the estimations of the services of the executive branch of authority. There is uncertainty in estimations.

A. EDUCATIONAL SERVICES CREATED BY THE EXECUTIVE BRANCH OF POWER

In the present time, a significant part of the establishments of the educational branch are financed from the budget. The population consumes these services free-of-charge. The national deputies, say that the expenses allocated from the budget for the educated of the people, create a hole in the budget. How can we explain such certainty of the national deputies?

On the one hand, it is connected with the interdiction, which existed in the realization of the research of the government's economic problems. On the other hand, it can also be attributed to the narrow-mindedness of the economists, who have been brought up on the economic theories of the last centuries.

Still, the productive activity of the educational branches is not examined in the theory. For this reason, the education services are badly taken into account in the productive part of the executive branch of authority.

The executive branch of authority should be taken into account in the results of not only receipts from the taxes, but also of the educational services which it creates. In the new (extended) variant of the calculations of the result of the economical activities of executive branch of authority (taking into account educational services), every goes into its proper place.

B. ENLIGHTENMENT SERVICES CREATED BY THE EXECUTIVE BRANCH OF POWER

Until recently, expenses, which are associated with the budget for enlightenment activity, were considered by many chiefs as «holes in the budget», which should be closed both on the right and left. Many academic economists recommend the reduction of expenses in the budget for enlightenment.

It is necessary to refuse such a traditional view, for the reason that the executive branch of authority does not take into account, in its results of economic activity, those services that create enlightenment. Today it is necessary to adjust the account of the services of enlightenment branches. Libraries, museums, the exhibition of representational and applied art, concert activity (national music, classical music, etc) are financed from the budget.

If the financing of the enlightenment branches occurs from the budget, the enlightenment services should be taken into account as a result of the activity of the executive branch of authority. Such consideration should be at the executive branch of authority.

This economic axiom of the executive branch of authority «number one.

C. THE SERVICES OF THE FIRST NATIONAL TELEVISION CHANNEL

In many countries, the services of the first national television and the first radio channels are financed from the budget. In this variant, it is necessary to take into account the service of these channels, as a result of the activity of the executive authority. If the first channel is financed from the budget, all the services of this information channel should also be taken into account in the total amount of the services of the executive branch of authority. The television service should be estimated taking into account the mastered resource of the free time of these services A_{STP}.

D. MISTAKES IN ECONOMIC ESTIMATES

In the economic theory of the intellectual sphere there is a paradox in the «logic»: museum visitors, cinema visitors, televiewers. There are examined without taking into account the time factor. From this context the following question arises:

How is it possible to investigate the economic processes in the intellectual sphere without considering the <u>duration</u> of visits to the establishments of Enlightenment and Entertainment institutions, etc?

Such a view in the theory leads to a deadlock. We need today new values, taking into account the resource of the spare time of the population and assimilated enlightenment services and entertainment services. [1]

I propose to consider the economic processes of the intellectual sphere, which include <u>temporary</u> components. The flow of visitors to museums, libraries, shows enterprises is a resource involved in the process of creating intellectual services. <u>In relation to this</u>, the population's spare time is also a resource component of intellectual services. We have no reasons to exclude this flow of resources from the calculations of economic estimations of intellectual services.

If we exclude the resource of the spare time of the population, the assimilated services of education, enlightenment and entertainment, in the results of economic activities of the executive power branches, then the economic processes may become distorted in our imagination. [2]

Thus, for example, the spare time of the population is not considered as an economic resource.

As a result of this subjective attitude, underestimations of the economic evaluations of the volume of intellectual services in the field of «education», «enlightenment» and «entertainment» take place.

This situation may logically remind one that when while calculating the volume of the transport service expenditure the cost of petrol is not taken into account.

---

1 Today in the economic theory that the «visitors» of museums, libraries and cinemas, television viewers, and radio listeners are considered as a statistic component of the general stream of resources.

2 It is possible to understand the economy of the intellectual sphere of a continent or a separate country only after creating a uniform system of economic estimation of indicators and utilization of resources.

But this is irrelevant to the sphere of the reduction of expenses and corresponds to the field of unaccounted resources.

The problem of resources has two sides to consider:

-conventional resources: fuel, electric power, material resources etc;

-unconventional resources:—the resources we know but do not economically estimate, and do not include in the cost of a newly made product, acting in a form of services.

In the branches of «education» there are the following streams of resources:

1) a stream of resources as means of labor and tools—work of art, books etc.—the stream estimated economically;

2) a stream of manpower—workers in the branches of «Education»—the stream estimated economically;

3) a stream of financial resources;

4) a stream of visitors is not considered an economic resource and is not estimated economically.

These problems are considered by author in the book: «The Macroeconomy of the Educational Sphere». In this book the author investigates the educational services in a three-dimensional space:

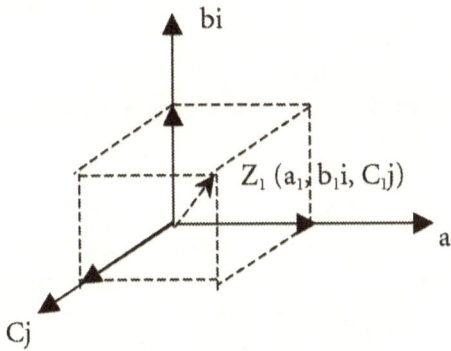

where

a is the past labor expenses involved in the creation of educational services;

bi is the direct labor expenses involved in the creation of educational services;

Cj is the «stream of students» assimilated by educational services.

$Z_1 = a1 + b1i + C1j$—Economic estimation of educational services.

Until recently the branches of «Enlightenment» and «Entertainment» have been operative in a range of «residual principle of financing», such attitude has not changed for years in most of countries. Economic science has carried out every possible zigzag, bypassing this area of human activity.

«Enlightenment» of people and «Entertainment» of people—these are continuously repeated processes bringing into motion certain elements: special means of labor and facilities of enlightenment (culture, art, religious) and entertainment (cinema, sport, TV, radio) branches, as well as application of special technologies. The principal thing about these two processes is that «visitors», «speculators» constitute a specific object of labor involved in the common stream of resource in the process of creation of intellectual values. Here you have «cultivating» of people by people.

In the branches of «enlightenment» there are the following streams of resources:

1) a stream of resources as means of labor and tools—work of art, books etc.—the stream estimated economically;
2) a stream of manpower—workers in the branches of «enlightenment»—the stream estimated economically;
3) a stream of financial resources;
4) a stream of visitors is not considered an economic resource and is not estimated economically.

Only if we have economic estimates on each of these four streams of resources can we setup real economic estimates and criteria of the results and effectiveness of economic activity in the enlightenment branches.

These problems can be encountered in the book: «The Macroeconomy of the enlightenment Sphere». In this book the author investigates the enlightenment services in a three-dimensional space:

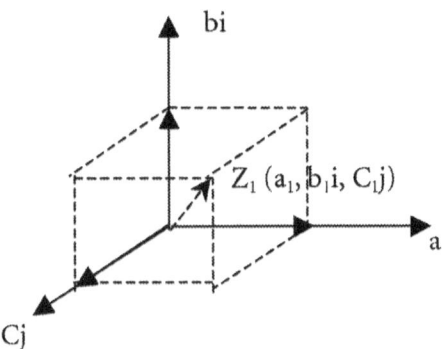

where

a is the past labor expenses involved in the creation of enlightenment services;

bi is the direct labor expenses involved in the creation of enlightenment services;

Cj is the «stream of students» assimilated by enlightenment services.

$Z_1 = a1 + b1i + C1j$—Economic estimation of enlightenment services.

The same situation happens in the «entertainment» branches. Here we have the following streams of resources:

1) a stream of resources as means of labor and tools—«entertainment»—the stream estimated economically;

2) a stream of manpower—workers in the branches of «entertainment»—the stream estimated economically;

3) a stream of financial resources;

4) a stream of visitors is not considered an economic resource and is not estimated economically.

These problems are considered by author in the book: «The Macroeconomy of Entertainment Sphere». In this book the author investigates the entertainment services in a three-dimensional space:

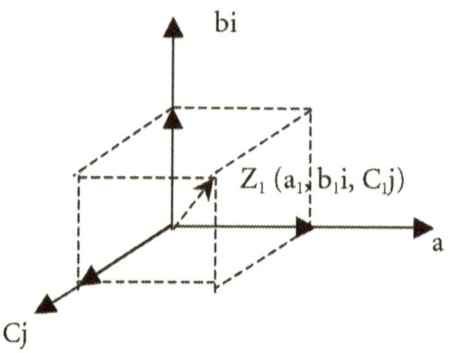

where
>   a is the past labor expenses involved in the creation of entertainment services;
>   bi is the direct labor expenses involved in the creation of entertainment services;
>   Cj is the «stream of visitors» assimilated by entertainment services.

$Z_1 = a1 + b1i + C1j$—Economic estimation of entertainment services.

The availability of economic estimations of each of these streams of resources will make it possible to really define economic estimations of the field of «enlightenment» and «entertainment», the criteria to determine their effectiveness in functioning.[3]

In the 21st century we should turn our heads to the economy of education and the economy of enlightenment. In these estimations, it is necessary to take into account the education services, enlightenment services, entertainment services which are financed by the budget.

---

3 The author investigates these problems in the book «The Economics: Enlightenment and Entertainment».

CHAPTER 2

ENLIGHTENMENT AND ENTERTAINMENT AS ECONOMIC SYSTEM

Today «enlightenment and entertainment branches» are a special part of the economy. It consists of an aggregate of enterprises and institutions, whose activities are directed towards servicing the population's spare time:

Subdivision A enlightenment branches:
- «Culture»—a network of museums, libraries and clubs.
- «Art»—a network of theatre, music, circus and concerts.
- «Religion branches»—a network of institutions (Orthodox, Catholic, Protestant, Muslim).

Subdivision B entertainment branches
- «Sports entertainment» branch.
- «Film distribution»—a network of cinema halls.
- «Radio Broadcasting»—a network of radio stations (both public and commercial).
- «TV Broadcasting»—a network of the TV stations (both public and commercial).[4]

---

4 Nowadays intellectual values and intellectual services have not found a reflection in economic theory. In particular: an essence of «intellectual value» is not formed; its economic properties are not clear; the borders of neither intellectual wealth nor its structure are established; neither is wealth estimated from a social and economic point of view. There is no unique scale of measuring its activities. Indeed the place of the «enlightenment and entertainment branches» is not clear. Its influence upon the

A lack of a considerable number of sections of economic theory means that the processes of the «enlightenment and entertainment branches» are frequently ignored. For example, how can it make sense that whole categories such as «Culture», «Art», «TV Broadcasting» and «Radio Broadcasting», etc. where millions of people work, are unprofitable for a State? How do we solve the contradiction between the requirement of increasing the intellectual welfare and a residual principle of financing this intellectual sphere?

People are a factor in required relations of the «enlightenment and entertainment branches», which correspond to different stages of development in productive intellectual forces. The aggregate of these specific economic relations makes up an economic structure of this intellectual sphere. This is the reality of what we reproduce every day.

The peculiarities of the economic relations in the «enlightenment and entertainment branches» categories are:

- *first,* **the process of creating (producing)** the «enlightenment and entertainment services» coincides with consumption;
- *second,* **the consumption process** is divided into two parts: production consumption and personal consumption;
- *third,* **the process of distribution** is the distribution of «enlightenment and entertainment services», and the results of these activities.
- *fourth,* **the process of exchange** is the type of relationship that exists between a seller and a buyer of «entertainment services» i.e., between «enlightenment and entertainment» enterprises and individuals, etc.

It is our opinion that an investigation of «enlightenment and entertainment» production must take the following directions:

- determine the peculiarities of the «enlightenment and entertainment branches» productive forces, i.e. means of labor, instruments of labor, subjects of labor and labor resources;
- analyze the peculiar features of economic relations in the «enlightenment and entertainment» branches, i.e.—production, distribution, exchange and consumption;
- reveal the contradictions in the development of productive forces and economic relations in the «enlightenment and entertainment branches» on the basis of a system of criteria to determine effective utilization of its resources.

---

aggregate of a society's activities is not elaborated—Gross Domestic Product, National Income, and the effectiveness criteria.

A. CHARACTER OF LABOR IN THE «ENLIGHTENMENT AND ENTERTAINMENT BRANCHES»

At present, economic theory is based on conception that only produces material values can be socially productive. Adherents of the theory believe that all socially arranged activities that lie beyond this definition are unproductive. Therefore they do not calculate labor results from the social production immaterial sphere into GDP, NDP, etc. For instance, one such adherent, Professor Livshitz A.L. notes, «the given type of labor is an unproductive one for society (i.e. the labor of a teacher, an actor, etc.)».[5]

It is a substantial (material) result that sets a criterion for the majority of researchers to distinguish between a productive and an unproductive character of labor. Labor is believed to be socially unproductive when the activity's result does not come out as a material value. It is our opinion that such an approach is not economic.

J.B. Sey criticized A. Smith on this matter 200 years ago. He proposed a broader concept of the category of «socially productive labor». He believed that any labor offering some definite usefulness, not only material, and presented, as a service was productive. In this context J.B. Sey is right to put the question: *«Why is all labor creating some usefulness not believed productive? Why should we refuse the labor of a teacher, who taught us all the skills that we earn money with now? Why should we give productivity to the labor of a pastry-cook, who makes sweets for our good tasting?»*

Furthermore, J. S. Mill, another representative of classical English political economics, scrutinized the problem. In particular, he noted *«a lot of authors refused to treat any labor as productive if there was not some material subject of its result that could passed from by one person to another»*. In other words, the question arises *«what is wealth and what is to be included in it: the material products only or all the useful products?...»* J. S. Mill accepts a broad treatment of productive labor that functions both in the material and other spheres of our social life.

While analyzing the labor process as a whole, J. S. Mill asserts that labor that creates some immaterial usefulness, which individuals' consumption is socially productive labor. He notes in particular: «In the given case labor is

---

5 A. L. Livshitz. Productive and Unproductive Labour in a Society.—Problems of an economic theory. p.88.

directed to give such specific features to people, that make them useful for themselves and for other people. The labor of all the people involved in the education process (teachers, tutors, professors and government employees) is the extent to which they wish to try and develop people. The labor of confessors and priests is also related to this type. The labor of doctors is also related, as doctors serve to sustain our lives; our physical and intellectual power. The labor of the people teaching others special professional skills, art and science as well as the labor of the students learning these skills and knowledge, are also related to the type.[6]

The time has forced a change of opinion on the socially arranged process of production. It could not be otherwise. The industrial structure of production has changed considerably in developed countries over the last 150 years. The service sector dominates material production in a proportion of 60 per cent to 40 per cent and 70 per cent to 30 per cent in some countries. The Gross Domestic Product (GDP) of the USA, Japan and other capitalist countries includes immaterial values alongside material values. This fact confirms that surplus labor in capitalist production is socially productive, irrespective of its material or immaterial result.

If we use the criterion, we can see that the number of employees and their assets in the branches of «Sports entertainment», «Culture», «Art», «TV Broadcasting» and «Radio Broadcasting» considerably increased in economically developed countries over the last 40 years. The expansion of these parameters is witness to the fact that arranged and organized rest brings profit. Economists calculated that the profit from investment in branches of the immaterial sphere was 2-2.5 times higher than the profit from investment in material production.

The character of labor in the «enlightenment and entertainment branches» is socially productive. There are a lot of examples that confirm that labor is profitable. For instance, the members of the «The Beatles», «Abba» and others, earned millions of dollars. They produced profitable «enlightenment and entertainment services» sold to people.

Together with the considerable number of the followers of the GDP cut structure there are followers of an expanded conception of GDP, which accounts for intellectual services. With increasing confidence they express what for many is an unusual opinion, namely *a requirement to include the labor results, which do not come out in a «material» form, into Gross Domestic Product (GDP) and National Income (NI).* Strumilin S.G., an academic, notes that «*the national income is usually calculated only in the material pro-*

---

6 A. Pigu. Economic Theory of Welfare, V.2, p.137

duction sphere, and the productivity of workers in this sphere is increased at the expense of employees in the other spheres...of science and culture. It would be a great mistake just to ignore their labor when calculating the whole expenses and achievements of a country».

A process of creating values and services, as such is dual. On the one hand, they are created within the framework of socially arranged production, and, on the other, they are created beyond it. For instance, making bread in a factory and at home are two equal processes as far as technology is concerned, but their principle of organization is different. Another example is the services of the «Enlightenment» branch at institutions and in private coaching. We can take these down in the scheme below:

DIALECTICAL SCHEME
OF SOCIALIZING PEOPLE'S ACTIVITIES

Thesis: Socially arranged process of producing values and services.
Antithesis: Socially unorganized process of producing values and services.
Synthesis: Aggregate process (both socially arranged and socially unorganized).

The above <u>social and personal principle of organizing this or that activity is a criterion,</u> which is a basis to determining a border line between productive and non-productive labor in the material and other spheres of a social body.

I believe that «socially productive labor» and «socially unproductive labor» are determined by the following objective economic criteria. <u>The first criterion</u> is welfare of the people. <u>The second criterion</u> is effectiveness of resource utilization and <u>the third criterion</u> is production of surplus value. If the labor process in the relatively autonomous spheres of production tells positively on changes to the values of the above stated economic criteria, this type of labor should be considered to be socially productive. Otherwise, the labor is socially unproductive.

The application of the above criteria allows us to set up a borderline, deciding which activity is socially productive or socially unproductive labor.

Having considered the problem of productive and unproductive labor in general, it is interesting to investigate it in the context of the relatively autonomous spheres of production: intellectual, «enlightenment and entertainment», military, public health, transport, administration and others.

The problem of the character of productive labor in the intellectual sphere remains open to debate by political economists. They still cannot decide whether to consider labor as socially productive or not.

Two different types of activity exist within the framework of the «enlightenment and entertainment branches». The first one is socially arranged within institutions; the second one operates outside the framework. The socially arranged and non-arranged intellectual servicing of people is in its organic unity an expansion of the borders of social activities by the intellectual sphere institutions, which leads naturally to a reduction of the second component, and vice versa.

An inter-connection of the processes can be set out in the scheme below:

DIALECTICAL SCHEME
OF SOCIAL ACTIVITIES IN PEOPLE'S SPARE TIME IN THE
«ENLIGHTENMENT AND ENTERTAINMENT BRANCHES»

Thesis: Socially productive character of labor in the «enlightenment and entertainment branches» (is labor arranged by a society to produce «enlightenment and entertainment services») aiming to assimilate the resource STP.

Antithesis: Socially non-productive character of labor is labor not involved in the socially arranged process of producing «enlightenment and entertainment services».

Synthesis: Aggregate labor in the «enlightenment and entertainment branches» is socially productive and socially non-productive labor.

In conclusion we can admit that the «enlightenment and entertainment» categories have developed considerably the last 40 years, and that the number of people involved in the process of intellectual servicing is increasing constantly. This is proof that social activities in people's spare time do not stay constant but continually expands their borders.

B. LABOR IN THE «ENLIGHTENMENT AND ENTERTAINMENT BRANCHES» (AS A PROCESS)

Labor in the «enlightenment and entertainment branches», first and foremost, is a process carried out between interacting factors: means and instruments of labor, a specific subject of labor (an individual or group) with the help of employees (musicians, actors, dancers, readers, priests etc.). Interaction of these factors is maintained in time and space consciously and purposefully. At the beginning of the process there is either a text of the speech or a score. The physical and intellectual power of the musicians and dancers, which determines, regulates and controls their activity, takes place during the entire process of labor. It is regulated by the technological settings of each entertainment production. An alteration of the knowledge, feelings and specific subjects of labor, who meet their own intellectual needs to a certain extent while being treated, takes place as before technological development.

The qualitative and quantitative character of the non-material-intellectual activity depends on the development of the factor-agents of the branches' productive forces. Each factor in the «enlightenment and entertainment» productive force bears definite social usefulness. Thus, if one of the factors in the productive force does not possess this property, the intellectual production is either impossible or imperfect.

We have clarified the general foundation of the labor process in assimilating people's spare time. Now we shall consider the interaction of these components of a specific labor process at a solitary level, using the following structural-functional model:

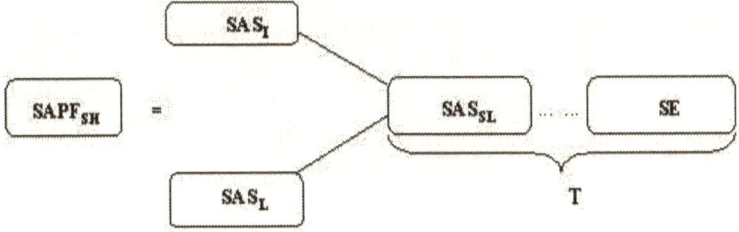

in which

SAPF$_{SH}$—an identifier of a solitary-aggregate productive force in the «enlightenment and entertainment branches»;

SAS$_I$—a solitary-aggregate system of labor resources

SAS$_L$—a solitary-aggregate system of instruments and means of labor;

SAS$_{SL}$—a solitary-aggregate system of labor subjects, i.e. an individual;

SE—a solitary employee;

T—time.

The above scheme reveals that the productive force in the «enlightenment and entertainment» categories is a unique system, whose elements are interconnected organically. A solitary-aggregate «enlightenment and entertainment service» is created as a result of this inter-action.

The above interactive process does not stand alone but aims to implement definite economic and social interests. The scheme is constructed on the basis of a systematic conception of the labor process. It is the required primary condition to calculate a mathematical-economic record of the process for each separate «enlightenment and entertainment» institution, the group and the category as a whole. The «enlightenment and entertainment» scheme clearly lines an interaction in the elements of its productive force.

The solitary factors or mono factors play a special role in the «enlightenment and entertainment» categories namely and in theatres, circuses, and in cinema.

It is not only the direct labor of the actors, musicians and so on, but also that the means and instruments of labor, as well as «enlightenment and entertainment services» are consumed while the solitary factors of this productive force interact with each other.

The creation of these services expends both past and direct labor of a lecturer and an actor—**simple and professional (complicated).**

The labor process has several varieties:

- When the labor subjects (individuals) are influenced with the help of natural investments of labor—speech—without using any electrical or mechanical instruments of labor.

- An electrified process of labor in the «enlightenment and entertainment branches», when people are treated to help from electrical equipment that strengthens vocal and musical influence.

CHAPTER 3

THE «ENLIGHTENMENT AND ENTERTAINMENT BRANCHES»

A. «ENLIGHMENT BRANCHES»

1. «CULTURE» AND «ART»

The branches of «Culture» and «Art» consist of museums, libraries, clubs, theatres, concert halls and circuses that target people's intellectual maturity.

«Culture» and «Art» have reached a considerable level of development. In the last 20 to 25 years the number of theatres increased by 26 per cent, the number of circuses by 33 per cent and the number of cinemas has by 46 per cent. A growth tendency in the total number of serviced viewers has take place in the last 25 years: An increase of 35 per cent in theatre-goers, of 54 per cent in concert goers; the number who go to circuses is up 2.1 times and cinema attendance has increased by 10 per cent.

Table 1 reveals that cultural and educational activity is given an important place in the aggregate socially-arranged process. Its capital assets are estimated to be hundreds of billions of dollars, the number of employees exceeded one million and the number of visitors amounted to hundreds of millions. One can see that it is a huge social-economic system.

In my opinion, the institutions of culture and art have not yet been considered by the theory of social-economic systems. This is the first point.

<u>Second</u>: the social-economic estimate of the activity results of institutions of culture and art have not yet been elaborated.

<u>Third</u>: there are no precise social-economic criteria of effectiveness with which to measure the activities of «Culture» and «Art» institutions. This leads to an indirect, method of determining the ways to improve their economic mechanism.

DEVELOPMENT OF THE «CULTURE» AND «ART» INSTITUTIONS IN THE LAST 25 YEARS

Culture institutions and types of cultural services	1	5	10	15	20	24	24% compare 1
Theaters	494	495	538	568	604	622	126
Circus enterprises	80	83	84	91	99	106	133
Museums of all government departments	929	954	1144	1295	1871	2021	218
Including art museums	114	119	134	144	173	257	225
Universal and popular libraries of all government departments number of libraries (thousands)	135.2	127.1	128.0	131.4	132.0	132.8	-2
Book funds (mln copies)	845.2	1097.7	1363.5	1607.8	1823.8	2048.6	242
Movie installations (thousands)	103.4	145.4	157.0	154.1	152.6	151.4	146
Visitors (million people)							
Theaters	90.9	100.8	110.2	115.7	119.2	122.5	135
Concerts	89.7	110.3	127.8	158.7	147.0	138.2	154
Circus	34.0	39.4	49.3	62.6	69.6	72.0	212

Museums of all government departments	49.8	75.0	102.8	134.4	156.4	180.9	363
Including art museums	11.4	19.0	28.8	39.1	44.4	44.0	386
Universal and popular librar-ies (book check out)	126.5	1196.6	1543.6	1950.2	2451.9	2573.3	251
Including func-tion	481.8	556.0	899.8	1078.5	1148.1	1398.9	290
Number of readers	53.0	62.5	77.7	94.5	112.0	116.2	219
Number of film shows	3611.0	4279.0	4652.0	4497.0	4252.0	3968.0	110

It is not possible to carry out a comparative analysis of the activities of different types of institutions because each branch uses a considerable number of indices and criteria. However, an analysis is possible, but only on one condition—we must consider the things that unite these enterprises and institutions, and not those that make them different. In my opinion, the unifying factors can be discerned from an economic basis only. The problems can be solved provided we break free from old and established ideas.

My research proceeds from the point that the main task of the accelerated development of the «Culture» and «Art» branches lies in their coordinated development as constituents of a unique social-economic system, i.e. of «enlightenment and entertainment branches». The problems of their complex development are as follows:

—a revelation of the economically profitable zones of servicing «Culture» and «Art» institutions in order to implement the branch resources most effectively.

—an economically rational redistribution of the «loading» between museums, libraries, clubs and theatres aiming to reach high social and economic results.

In our opinion, solving the problems must start with a clarification of what the solitary process of interaction of «enlightenment and entertainment» process factors, really is.

—An individual and population are subjects of labor in «Culture» and «Art». Cultural activities are not possible with out an individual—without an object for the activity to be directed onto. The activity is aimless if a specific subject of labor is absent in the cultural and educational process.

—The employees that possess definite professional skills and methods of «treating» individuals in the process of cultural servicing can be considered as «labor resources» for the «Culture» and «Art» branches.

—Word, sound, musical instruments, musical equipment, books and pictures are «instruments of labor». «The instruments of labor» stand between specific cultural labor resources and specific subjects of labor.

A system for the interaction of solitary means and instruments of labor, solitary labor resources and solitary subjects of labor in «Culture» and «Art» can be set out as follows:

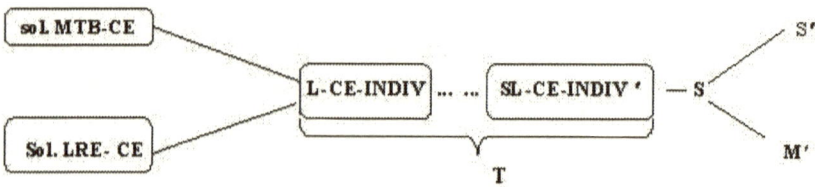

in which:

sol. MTB—CE—solitary means of labor of the cultural activity;

sol. LRE—CE—solitary employee of the cultural activity;

L-CE-INDIV—subject of labor in the cultural activity;

SL-CE-INDIV'—subject of labor—an individual influenced by the cultural activity;

T—time taken by the process of interaction between solitary factors of production, during which a solitary cultural service is created.

The above model of the productive force behind «Culture» and «Art» reflects what generally takes place in every production process—the expedient interaction of production factors in order to create a service.

An organizer of «enlightenment and entertainment» enterprise purchases (buys or rents) capital assets employs «labor resources» and enlists other factors required for production, to start the production of «enlightenment and entertainment» services. ***They are consumed freely—S or for money—M.***

MUSEUMS

The «Museum» system has reached considerable dimensions, clear from its statistic data.

The basis for this system is:
—a principle of integrity
—a principle of interaction between the system's components, etc.

However, what is absent is economic principle, which I believe must be evidence in the material and intellectual development of the people. The lack of economic principle in the organization, planning and management of museums has caused considerable social-economic damage to the intellectual sphere of our society, especially in the late 1920s, when a great many monuments were impaired—far more than during the Second World War. In addition to decades of bad management, inadequate funding of restoration projects has had a negative effect on the state of their preservation.

Analyzing the publications written about museum problems, it is clear that there are few articles that tackle employee incentives, questions of organization, planning and the characteristics of applying economic leverage to the management of those institutions. This is because many economic-scientists do not regard the «Museum» system as a primary economic theory.

Many theoretical questions about the development of this branch have yet to be worked out:
-the total indicators of museum planning have not changed since the 1920s
-there is an imperfect distribution of museums round the country
-output of museum activities is not calculated from a social and economic point of view
-the characteristics of economic relations within the museum branch have not been worked out.

The above shortcomings of research into questions of museum development begs the following questions:
-what is the essence of the economic development strategy for the «Museum» system if available estimates are not used?
-if there is a lack of resource criteria, are museum resources being used rationally?

The answers to these questions are unequivocal—an absence of adequate indicators and criteria have had a negative effect on the quality of museum development. Only three per cent of museum funds are exposed, while the remaining 97 per cent are stored as dead weight in reserve. Such irrational waste of material and intellectual values in a society is harmful from both a social and an economic point of view.

MUSEUMS AS PRODUCTIVE FORCE

If museum institutions are considered as a social and economic system, we should consider their components in more detail. A museum institution is made up from a number of different parts. These components are grouped into a <u>material-substantial group</u> of factors (buildings, constructions, pictures, etc.); labor resources (museum employees, research officers, administration and servicing staff) are the <u>second group</u> of factors and museum visitors are a <u>the third factor.</u> In these three elements, factor and resource interact in time and space, as services are created and consumed.

An interaction of these factors can be set out as follows:

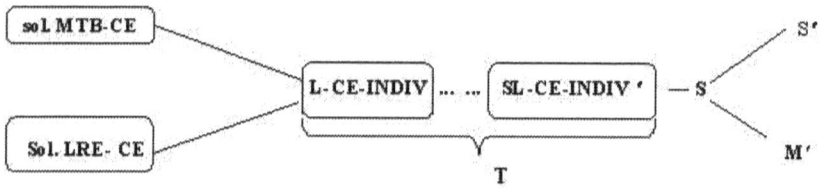

sol. MTB—CE—solitary means of labor of the museum system;
sol. LRE—CE—solitary employee of the museum system;
L-CE-INDIV—subject of labor in the museum system;
SL-CE-INDIV'—subject of labor—an individual influenced by the museum system;
T—duration of servicing an individual.

Each element of the system is capable of executing a specific museum function as a part of, and not separates to the entire system. If capital assets and visitors are absent, then museum services are not created.

LIBRARIES

The analysis of statistics «enlightenment and entertainment» that total indicators used in libraries has not changed for many decades. Such constancy «enlightenment and entertainment» that they are either universal or stagnant in the theoretical approach to organizing and planning the library business. Target indicators, as they stand reflect the process of creating library services inadequately. As a result, management and planning only have a formal responsibility for the economic process of the «Library» branch. The indicators therefore set out a considerably disproportionate development of fixed capital, labor forces and distribution of library services among different social-demographic population groups.

Library methods of management are 100 per cent administrative-commanding. Economic stimulation of workers' labor is absent here.

The scale of development in the «Library» branch is rather significant. 234,000 libraries contained 2,165 million books and magazines, worth tens of billions dollars. The number of «Library» employees exceeded 500,000. In one year, 250 million people visited libraries.

The figures given above «enlightenment and entertainment» that the «Library» branch is a large-scale economic system. It is called to satisfy the people's reading needs, broaden and educate people, creating favorable conditions for a harmonious intellectual development of people and offering them a rational use of their spare time.

Unfortunately, this is subject to the negative peculiarity of the present structure of management methods' applied to the «Library» branch.

Researching the problems in the «library» business exposes the necessity of working out and putting into practice new methods of organization and management, based on social-economic criteria that allow us to conduct an analysis of social-economic trends in this branch.

But exactly what problems are in question that need to be worked out?

In my opinion they are as follows:

   -research into the character of economic relations—the process of creation, distribution, exchange and consumption of library services

   -research into the field of social-economic estimates of library products

   -working out questions about the prospective social-economic effectiveness of the branch's development

   -processing a social-economic model of current and long-term development planning of library institutions

   -investigating the current and long-term structure of people's demand for library services.

We must not only the expenditures on material and financial resources and the labor forces in library institutions, but we must be able to distribute them optimally in time and space and make rational use of an economic incentive to boost effectiveness of library functioning.

LIBRARIES AS A PRODUCTIVE FORCE IN SOCIETY

When we consider the economic processes in people's library service, a special place is given to informational modeling carried out by mathematical and logical methods.
The process of library service is an interaction of:
-means and instruments of labor in the libraries (books, etc.);
-librarian staff (LIB-STAFF);
-subjects of labor-readers.

The interaction of the above stated factors is not carried out by itself but aims to implement definite economic and social interests. An organizer of the library process acts as according the scheme below:

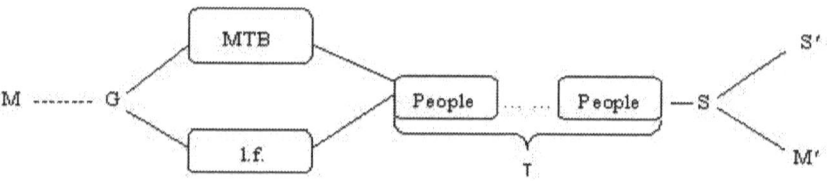

These three constituents interact directly between themselves. A librarian accelerates a process by searching for the required books. The material and intellectual bearers of information are instruments of influence upon individuals (readers). In turn, a reader is «a subject» on to which influence is directed. In this interaction, library services are created.

2. «RELIGION INSTITUTIONS»

ORTHODOX SYSTEM

In Russia «Church» was a huge and powerful social-economic force before the 1917 Revolution. There were nearly 1,300 monasteries and 80,000 churches. Church services were produced and exchanged for material values donations. Considerable returns came from an agricultural sector, where thousands of clerics, lay brothers and sisters and others worked. It should be noted that the Russian Church always had taxation privileges. Even at the time of the Mongolian invasion, Church lands and property were not pillaged and free from paying taxes to the Horde. Consequently a lot of big land-owners (boyars and small princes) used to give property and land to the Church, adding to its strength as a social-economic force administrated by the Synod.

In October 1917 religious ideology was thrown into direct conflict with communist ideology. A competitive struggle for spheres of influence took shape in the market of intellectual services. The communists used all available means, the most radical of which was the physical elimination of 160,000 Church servants.

«The October Revolution served as both prologue to and cause of the destruction of orthodox monasteries, bringing with it the first decrees of the new power. A liquidation program under the «Narkomat» of justice was set up in 1918. The propaganda machine, picking up pace in its activities, was quickly able to stir up hatred among large numbers of people towards monasteries and initiate mass demands to confiscate their treasures. The authorities were consciously destroying piety in millions of people. Within a few days, monuments of priceless intellectual, historical, artistic and material value, from almost all shrines in Russia were confiscated, taken to the «Gohran» or museums. Thousands of pounds of silver were taken out of the monasteries to special warehouses and from there to the Moscow «Gohran». Eighty four pounds from Salovets monastery, 57 pounds from Chudov monastery, 28 from Spassk-Andronnikov's and 25-26 from Simonov, Vosnesensk and Davidov monasteries. The least resistance was used as an excuse to unleash terror against clergymen. The monasteries that were closed down, housed, according to the «Revolution and Church» magazine Calculation, 349 hospitals, 287 Soviet military institutions of the (mostly military units) and 14 concentration camps. Those converted into concentration camps in Moscow were, Spassko-Andronov, Novospassk and Ivanov monasteries. Against all these «deeds», the created monastery museums seemed quite inconspicuous. The list had been reduced to 60 by 1922, 14 of which were in Moscow and the Moscow region (Podmoscovie). And in only a score of monasteries was it possible to set up museums anyway after the nationalization of land, landless monasteries were occupied by children's colonies, orphanages, etc.[7]
Monks had to leave monasteries and wander fields. In the late 20's the dismantling of a number of historic monasteries took on mass proportions. Monastery cemeteries were razed to the ground. Granite and marble tombstones were used

7 Monasteries of Russia in the first years after the Revolution. Journal of the Moscow Eparchy, 1993, № 4.

to build monuments of Lenin. Bells were also designed, carried out according to the orders. **In 1930 the greatest bell in Russia, belonging to Troitsko-Sergievsko-Lavra, weighing 67 tones, was recast. But the most terrible event was the complete demolishing of shrines and church towers. Still no historic research has been conducted, nor there is a clear picture of the vandalism.**

Monasteries such as Chudov's, Vosnesensky, Simonov's, Nikitsky, Zachatievsky, Sretensky, Strastnoy, Michaelovsky, Latoverhny in Kiev, Bryansky, Svensky, Spasso-Kamenny were completely or almost completely demolished.

From the second half of the 70s onwards, the desecration of objects in churches took on an unprecedented scale; only an infinitesimal part of them were put in museums.

City and regional finance departments dispatch church property to warehouses. For utilization, they valued square meter of gilded <u>icon</u> at one ruble, a ton of non-ferrous metal—670 rubles, one kilogram of silver—30 rubles, church attires embroidered with gold and silver from two—to three rubles for one kilogram. It took the new regime only one and a half decades to destroy centuries of cultural heritage of Great Russia. The intellectual and material losses were so great, that it could only have affected the people's moral health. Russia, as a Valaam monk wrote, «is committing suicide».

The interaction process of factors in a church institution looks, in general, as below:

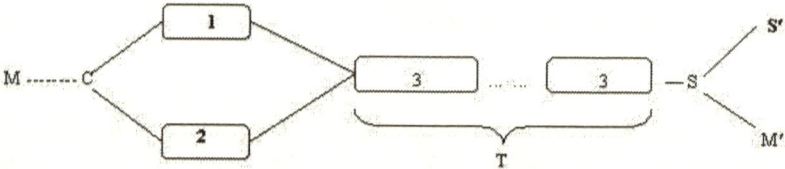

in which

    1—Church buildings, church utensils, etc.

    2—Church labor resources (priests, etc.);

    3—Church visitors

    T—Duration of servicing an individual in the Church.

There are more than enough foundations upon which to consider the Church as a branch of intellectual production. Its capital assets are estimated at many billions of dollars, and there are thousands of people working in the Church system. The income from its activities is great. Here, we are confronted with a large social-economic system.

Each element of the system is capable of executing a basic Church function within the frames of the entire given system and not on its own. No services are produced if there are no visitors.

The Church system has two basic targets:
- Production of services to assimilate a resource for people's spare time
- Involvement of people in the process of servicing to exchange specific intellectual services for material values, in the form of donations.

If an economist considers Church services as an economist, he would draw up the following system:

Get married—to be crowned,
Baby born—to be baptized,
House built—to be blessed,
Man died—the burial service to be read,
Absolution required—the absolution given.

In other words, the Church is present at all our celebrations and family occasions. Church services, for sure are not free. There is «a tariff» for every type of church service. There is one price in building the Church, and another price when going out.

Today Churches in Russia have the following targets:
- strengthening its material basis. First and foremost is the return of church property that was confiscated during communist rule. (In case confiscated property is not available, the state must cover the losses with the well-known paintings that depict Church themes)
- returning Church land.

CATHOLIC SYSTEM

THE VATICAN AS AN ECONOMIC SYSTEM[8]

The Vatican is the smallest state in the world, situated on the hill of Monte-Vatican, in the western part of Rome, taking up slightly more then 44 hect-

---

8 Velukovich L.N. «Catholicism in the present world».

ares of land. The constant population of this state is just over a thousand. Its unchallenged ruler is the Pope head of the Roman Catholic Church.

Despite the modest size of the Pope's residence, the power, wealth and influence of the Catholic Church in the modern world are quite tangible. Land, which belongs to the Church in Italy, Spain and other countries, bring in a constant and substantial income. However, the primary income of the Vatican comes from its sphere of «enlightenment and entertainment» business.

The city-state issues its own stamps and coins with the Pope's profile and owns radio stations. The largest of them—«Vatican Radio» transmits in 45 languages. The radio station «Veritas»—one of the most powerful in the world, serves Asia. The church publishes a large number of periodicals, daily newspapers, weekly magazines, etc.

According to data produced by the Vatican statistics bureau, the Catholic Church produces and owns 5,000 different editions putting the total number of printed copies at about two million per annum, including 53 daily newspapers. There are 755 weekly magazines and about 2,000 monthly magazines. 93.5 per cent of these editions are national. «Familia Christiana» magazine (Christian family) has the largest circulation: 26 million in the USA and 12 million in Germany.

The church adopts modern methods of influence on parishes with the aid of «enlightenment and entertainment» business. For instance, they have managed to preserve a network of cinemas belonging to parishes in Italy, by lowering ticket prices below those charged by other cinemas.

Special attention is paid to TV. Here the church does not save on means, paying T.V companies to highlight primary aspects of Catholic life.

The Salesian Order undertakes work in developing countries. They have set up 600 schools and 300 vocation colleges, including a center for pedagogic and social communication problems.

A relatively new Catholic Order called «Opus den» (God's business) was set up in Spain in 1928. The primary principle is that the structure list of the Order's members, the contents of its 479 articles of regulations and all kinds of the Order's activities are kept a well guarded secret. The «Opus den» is a secular institution. Its members live as laymen, penetrating all spheres of human activities. The order takes an active part in business, controlling the activities of a network of banks, construction companies and industrial firms. It influences the activities of 500 universities, 700 periodical, 60 radio and T.V stations and 12 film studios. The Order owns firms engaged in film and videocassette distribution. Trains businessmen, economists and sociologists. As a result, its members penetrate all branches of the secular world, keeping their membership in the Order secret.

Despite tremendous efforts to keep its parishioners faithful, the church will not be able to present the global crisis in religious consciousness, which is spreading over not only Catholicism, but also all other traditional religions. It manifests itself in a reduction of the number of active church followers and the rise of a substitute belief system in external manifestations. The number of church goers is in decline. Only 10 per cent of those who call themselves Catholic go to mass. Aware of the necessity of intensifying its activities among the youth, the Church has set up so called intellectual centers, at educational institutions and elsewhere. These centers' tasks were established by the Second Vatican Cathedral (1962-1965). «It is necessary to create centers in a community or church, where an individual is able to have his or her intellectual needs satisfied: These centers, according to existing conditions, can take different forms—associations, sections, sessions for intellectual development, so that each person can stop feeling lonely...». The spare time of youth became a massive focus of attention. In order to draw youth into religion, the Church sets up Catholic sports unions. For instance, the Catholic sports center in Italy unites about half a million sportsmen. The Church invests considerable sums to develop and maintain bases. In its possession are over 300 gymnastic grounds, about 1,500 football fields, 800 tennis courts, more than 2,000 volleyball and 1,500 basketball courts. If the youth do not go to Church—the Church will go to the youth. The famous football clubs (Milan, Kalliary, Lazzio and others), have been taken under the Church's protection.

The Vatican is the owner and keeper of the greatest cultural and artistic masterpieces of human genius. The list of treasures starts at «main entrance» to the Vatican—St. Peter's Square is decorated with 284-meter columns. All are decorated with figures of the saints carved in stone. St. Peter's Cathedral is the largest Catholic temple in the world, taking almost a hundred years (1506-1625) to build under such architects as Michelangelo, Bramante, Jakomo Della Porte and others. The Cathedral is decorated inside with paintings by Michelangelo, Pieta marble (morning over), <u>Baldwin</u> bronze and tombstone works by Bernini, and other outstanding Italian sculptors. To the north of the Cathedral spreads the enormous palace ensemble, created in XV-XVI EC. The remarkable Italian painters of the Italian Renaissance stanzas by Raphael, paint the walls of the palace, Penturiccio designs Borgia's apartments, in Nick's V chapel there are murals by Michelangelo, Botticelli, Perugino and others. Besides the palaces and chapels of greatest art value, their museums contain priceless treasures. Unique are the museums of antique sculpture (Pio-Clementino and Chianti), in which artifacts from Egypt, Etruss, Ellyn and Roman culture have been collected.

There is an enormous library with a unique collection of books and ancient manuscripts, a large number of which have hardly been read due to their reprohonsibleness (according to church censorship). The Vatican picture gallery—Menomonee is yet another separate building.

Income from tourists visiting the Vatican's palaces and museums provide a constant and notable part of church incomes: this sphere of «enlightenment and entertainment» business is never-ending, since the unique cultural art values belonging to the Vatican will be human magnets forever.

B. «ENTERTAINMENT BRANCHES»

1. «SPORTS ENTERTAINING»

A sport is an ancient form of entertainment that some people prefer to material benefit. Sport contests and matches give their spectators the joy of excitement, of reveling in a sportsman's victory or luck—precisely is what people can miss so badly in their own day to day life.

Sport has long since grown into a gigantic sphere in advanced countries. Thus, in 1988, the absolute gross product of USA's sport industry amounted to 63.1 billion dollars, including:

• sport recreation and health improvement activity	22.8 billion dollars
• production of sports equipment	1.9 billion dollars
• selling tickets for sports contests	3.2 billion dollars
• golf clubs	8.0 billion dollars
• recreational clubs of tennis, racquetball and squash	6.3 billion dollars
• aquatic recreation	4.7 billion dollars
• bowling and billiard clubs	2.0 billion dollars
• other kinds of sports-health-improvement activity	1.8 billion dollars

From the given above figures it is clear that the sports business in the USA is filled with a great number of stadiums, edifices and firms producing «enlightenment and entertainment» services. Organization of such a branch, which would annually produce services and products that amount to over 60 billion dollars, is long and complex, both in its formation and its development as an economic system.

The process of interaction of «enlightenment and entertainment» factors in
   sports production is not put into practice unpurposefully, but realizes certain economic and social interests.
An organizer of «enlightenment and entertainment» enterprise acts according
   to the scheme set out below:

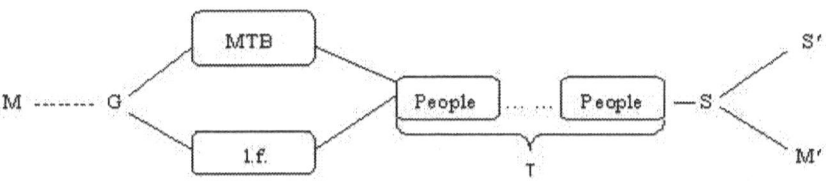

Possessing a certain amount of money, an organizer of «enlightenment and
   entertainment» enterprise purchases the necessary factors of production:
   - material and technical base (MTB): sports edifices, stadiums (or rents
     them);
   - employs sportsmen, football players and begins to produce «enlighten-
     ment and entertainment» services.

As a result of the process, a sport service (football, tennis, etc.) is being created,
   which is consumed by people free of charge (S') or for money (M').
Professional businessmen make sports look especially spectacular. This excit-
   ing performance is staged according to the laws of profit, especially when
   the game in question gathers billions of spectators such as football world
   championships or the Olympic games.
The Olympic games bear all the traits of ordinary business. The American NBC
   Company paid 300 million dollars just to transmit the 1998 winter Olympic
   Games in Calgary. A net profit of 250 million dollars made by the city of
   Los Angeles stimulated 13 other cities to bid to host the Olympic games in
   1992. What all contenders were interested in, were profits and multi-million
   dollar transactions.
Sports business is seizing the world. Taking part are sports functionaries, man-
   agers and sportsmen themselves, as well as owners of has become the mass
   media, politicians and businessmen. Football is a partially good example. It
   has become a profitable business. The buying and selling of football players
   and whole teams, to compete with monopoly companies inevitably causes
   «elite» sportsmen and clubs to appear, which top the league year after year.

They make big money. In 1985 the monthly salary of a top class international player was a substantial 50 thousand dollars. By 1990 it has risen to 100 thousand dollars. Now it has reached 150 thousand dollars.

It takes big money to obtain good football players today. If a club manages to invest its capital successfully, it will begin to win matches, the number of fans will grow and the club's financial position will improve. The club will be able to buy new stars, who in turn will bring the club new victories and increase capital. Money, as always, continues to buy victory. It takes big money, as it did before, to win matches. But while on a winning streak one has to spend ever larger amounts of money in order to keep one's position at the top. Economic law clearly applies here.

Skyrocketing prices for football players, match services and publicity expenditures mean that only rich cities can afford them. As a result, a new division in sports labor appears: **on the one hand,** clubs spring up with the opportunity to become champions; **on the other hand**—small clubs still exist, but their destiny boils down mostly to preparing players for leading clubs.

The trend in the French football is to strive to bring its champions' earnings in line with those of the leading countries in this sphere. But some question why the taxpayers should have to bear the brunt of the exercise earnings of football players, when they might not ever be football fans.

The French Football Federation and the National Football League answer that they serve society, entertaining between 5 to 6 million people each Sunday. We educate the youth, otherwise lost because of high unemployment and give «the spirit of sport» meaning to their existence: there are 22,000 clubs, 100,000 volunteer organizers and 1,750,000 sportsmen including 20,000 women—all this costs several millions of francs of state subsidy. The Paris Opera alone costs the state 20 million francs a year; a famous conductor can earn 20,000 dollars in an evening.

2. «FILM DISTRIBUTION»[9]

The year 1995 turned out to be as successful as 1994 for the Buena Vista company. Not only did it top the list of income in the USA film market, but it also earned over a billion dollars from distributing film in the USA and Canada. Warner Brothers, as last year, was in honorable second place, while Sony spurted through the last weeks of 1995 and thus managed to take third place. Buena Vista, Walt Disney's film distributor, received an income of one billion, ten million dollars, almost as much as its income in 1994. It should

---

9 The Hollywood Reporter (World of entertainment, № 3, 1996)

be noted that before 1994 no US Company ever exceeded the billion-dollar barrier income. In total the American film companies made a profit in the region of 5 billion and 510 million dollars in 1995. A rise in ticket prices meant that they sold in smaller quantities than in the previous year. In 1995, a total of 1.28 billion tickets were sold. That was two per cent less than the total of sales of 1994, when 1.29 billion tickets were sold. The sum total of film distribution in 1994 was 5.4 billion dollars. Only seven films in 1995 exceeded the income barrier of a hundred million, taking into account the sum total of film distribution in the USA and Canada. The greatest hit of last year was Warner Brothers' «Batman Forever», which collected nearly 184 million dollars. Ten films exceeded an income barrier equal to 100 million dollars in 1994, including two, which collected 300 million dollars each. These were «Paramount»'s «Forrest Gump» and «Buena Vista»'s «The lion King». These films took third and fifth place respectively in the level of received incomes in the entire history of the US film market. The 1994 hit «Batman Forever» was followed by the 1995 hits «Apollo 13» (Universal, $172.1 million), «Toy Story» (Buena Vista, $150 million), «Pochahontas» (Buena Vista, $141.5 million), «Ace Ventura: When Nature Calls» (Warner Brothers, $105 million), «Casper» (Universal, $100.3 million), «Die Hard With Avengeance» (20th Century Fox, $ 100.1 million). All figures are based on the total income from film distribution in the USA and Canada reached on January 1, 1996.

The top ten of 1995 collected a total of 1.23 billion, $352 million (22 per cent) less than the total of income of the top ten films of 1994. The top 25 distribution hits of 1995 made a total of $2.28 billion some $322 (12 per cent) less then the comparable total for 1994 that amounted to $2.61 billion. Expert opinion maintained that the films of 1995 were less entertaining. That is why only seven of them exceeded 100 million in income. Besides, it is well known that income from films grow and contract in cycles, each cycle lasting approximately 3-4 years. Revenue of 1.15 billion tickets sold was 1991 income growth from film distribution in the US and Canada, at least in the near future, is predicted to be held up. According to long-standing observations, such stagnation usually lasts from a year, to a year-and-a-half.

THE SHARE DISTRIBUTION OF PROFITS FROM FILM DISTRIBUTION AMONG US FILM-COMPANIES

Name of film company	1993		1994			1995		
	No. of films	Share %	No. of films	Share %	Company rating	No. of films	Share %	Company rating
1. Buena Vista	34	16,60%	37	19,70%	2	39	19,40%	1
2. Warner Brothers	35	18,90%	39	16,40%	1	31	16,60%	2
3. Sony	-	-	-	-	-	34	13,10%	-
4. Universal	21	14,20%	23	12,60%	3	21	12,70%	4
5. Paramount	14	9,50%	20	14,20%	6	24	10,10%	3
6. Fox	21	10,90%	18	9,40%	5	15	8,00%	5
7. New Line	27	3,70%	27	7,00%	8	29	6,60%	6
8. MGM/UA	12	1,90%	11	2,80%	10	18	6,30%	10
9. Miramar	24	3,10%	28	3,90%	9	42	3,60%	9
10. Savoy	2	0,40%	6	1,40%	16	10	1,30%	12
11. Gramercy	6	0,70%	13	1,90%	12	15	1,10%	11

3. «TV BROADCASTING» AND «RADIO BROADCASTING»

In the USA, «TV Broadcasting» consists of 728 commercial stations, 256 non-commercial ones, three TV networks and 200 million TV sets. «Radio Broadcasting» includes 5,000 stations, 3,000 FM stations, 1,000 stations of public broadcasting, 4 commercial networks, 1 network of public broadcasting, and 500 million radio sets.

A high rate of development of the technical means of receiving and transmitting information conditioned a further broadening of the influence of «TV Broadcasting» and «Radio Broadcasting» in the 80s and 90s. The speedy development of networks of TV-and Radio-centres creates mega-groups in both vertical and horizontal sectors—including information empires that units Radio and TV.

These superpowers still face the problems that are connected with determining particular niche in «enlightenment and entertainment service» market, among which the basic ones are:

-establishing a share of this or that mega-group in the total volume of «enlightenment and entertainment service» production

-researching current and long-term «demand» for «enlightenment and entertainment services»

-investigating effective utilization of resources informational mega-group

Without the above knowledge it is difficult to find out where, when and at what volume, it is expedient to invest in the development of radio and TV broadcasting networks and stations.

To answer the question above, we must look at «TV Broadcasting» and «Radio Broadcasting» from an economic point of view, a novel approach for these categories.

AN ANALYSIS OF «TV» AND «RADIO BROADCASTING» MODELS

A formulaic approach to the development of economic theory was widely disseminated in the 1970s. Its essence lied in efforts to formalize economic processes and trends in «TV Broadcasting» and «Radio Broadcasting».

Pal Tamash's model is determined by a production function, worked out by Kobe and Douglas. In his version it appears as follows:

$$G = A \cdot L^{\alpha} \cdot C^{1-\alpha}$$

where
   A, are constants, whose value depends on competitive social interactions.

Designating **w** as a provisional part of a national product to expand the mass
   information sphere. It determines an efficiency indicator as follows:

$$E = \eta \frac{w \cdot G}{N}$$

in which
   E—average labor efficiency,
   N—size of working population;
   η—average functional efficiency of mass information means' effect.[10]

On the basis of the above Cobb-Douglas modification production function is
   written as follows:

$$G = A \cdot \eta \cdot (w \cdot G)_0 \, \alpha \cdot (l \cdot G)_0 \, \alpha$$

G_0 in the right part of the equation is GDP of inverse relationship. Proceeding
   from the fact that G0 was created in preceding cycle, Pal Tamash derived the
   following equation:

$$l = \frac{G}{G_0} A \times \eta \times wa$$

Solving the task of determining the extreme value of this functional, we derived
   the following optimal values:

$$W \, \text{опт} = \frac{\lambda}{A_\eta^\alpha} \left(\frac{\alpha}{1 - \alpha} \right)^{1-\alpha}$$

---

10 Book «Mass communication in socialist society». p.77, 83-85.

$$C \text{ опт} = \frac{\lambda}{A_{\eta}^{\alpha}} \left(\frac{1 - \alpha}{\alpha} \right)^{\alpha}$$

Maximally the functional G appears as follows:

$$G_0 (c + S) = l \cdot G_0 \cdot \left[1 - \frac{\lambda}{A_{\eta}^{\alpha}} \left(\frac{\alpha}{1 - \alpha} \right)^{1 - \alpha} \right.$$

The above formulas, according to Pal Tamash will allow us to come to the following conclusions:

- «*firstly, optimizing social purposes, keeping under control capital and intellectual (educational, cultural, informational) investment results in the optimal growth of a national product, which may be planned and maximized (the task of searching for optimal value 1);*
- «*secondly, growth in social profit (income), may result in an increase in efficiency of the cultural sphere as well*».

Pal Tamash has not determined an economic structure of «enlightenment and entertainment service» and its division into expense and income portions. His mathematical models miss the assimilated resource of people's spare time.

Along with the mathematics, some authors used graphic models and figures. Thus, for instance, professor Alexeev proposes the following model:

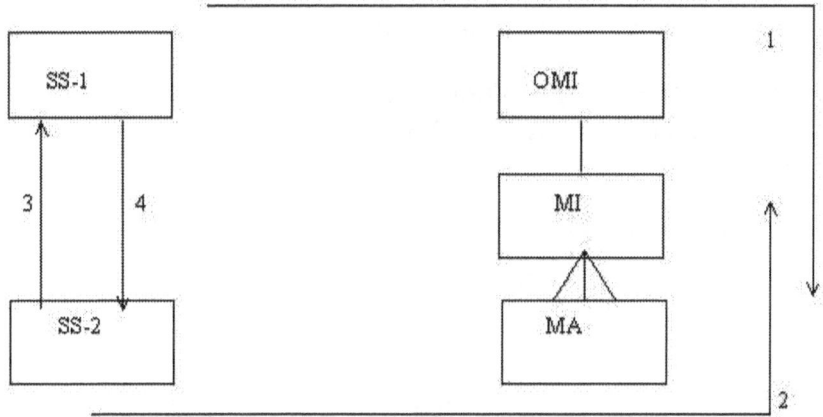

Model of mass communication.

in which

    SS-1—social subject 1,
    SS-2—social subject 2,
    OMI—organ of mass information,
    MI—mass information,
    MA—mass audience,
    1—the direction of the activity of social subject 1
    2—the direction of the activity of social subject 2
    3-4—system of relations between social subject 1 and 2.[11]

Professor M.D. Kozlenko considers questions of method and techniques in studying the means of mass information according to the following structure:

1)   system presentation of intellectual benefits
2)   mass information as a subsystem of a system of intellectual benefits
3)   analysis and synthesis of a system of forming factors
4)   stratification of general totality by several parameters of a communicative character.

Professor. M.D. Kozlenko ascertains that the movement of what is carried out in many aspects «by processes as well as by stages of reproduction». One of the chief problems of the sociology of intellectual benefits, in the authors opinion, is the «*creation of a special configuration of the intellectual benefit system's movement as a dynamic model and a row of configuration by separate stages of reproduction, as static models of production and storage, passing on spreading consumption of intellectual benefits, supply and demand for them*». Then M.D. Kozlenko noted that the «*configuration of factors forming the consumption of mass information in mainly…for building a proper dynamic model as the global task of the sociology of mass communications*».

Many indicators characterize consumption of mass information. The main ones are as follows:

• character of consumed information
• informational concentration (from a theoretical and informational point of view)
• structure of mass communications in given co-ordinates
• information at the moment of consumption

---

11 «Social problems of intellectual life». p. 52, 53.

• individual level of consumption of information (in time) (V).[12]

Professor M.D. Kozlenko then considers necessary and sufficient building conditions on the basis of the above five indicators model of dimensional distribution. He remarked that the «*application of factor analysis...allows the
   building of several **n-1** dimensional models or receiving of several appropriate
   kinds of factors solutions during the processing of specific mass information...
   The latter of the given indicators (V), for a number of reasons, plays a special
   role in setting and solving the indicated problems*».
However, he does not give a formulaic record of **n-l** dimensional economic and
   mathematical models in the sphere of mass information, which makes it
   impossible to determine their level of adequacy in the actual process of this
   subsystem development of social production.
In the schematic form interaction of the system of mass information with other
   communications is as follows:

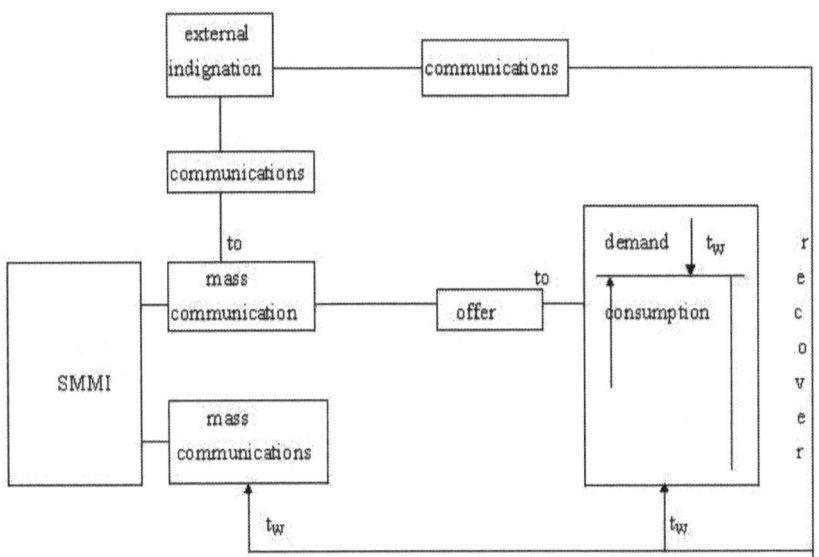

Informational and chronological presentation of the V-system

SMMI—system of the means of mass information

---

12 «Methodological problems of a long-term planning for a culture development»
(Collection of articles), p.12.

to and t_W—time of the effect of the V-system at the moment of mass information consumption.

THE BRANCHES OF «TV BROADCASTING» AND «RADIO BROADCASTING» AS A PRODUCTIVE FORCE IN SOCIETY

Solution of the economic problems faced by «TV Broadcasting» and «Radio Broadcasting» must begin by clarifying the essence of the process of interaction between the factors of this special production. The following participate in it:

- Labor resources of «TV Broadcasting» and «Radio Broadcasting» are personnel, program presenters, actors and people who possess definite professional skills and methods of «treating» TV viewers and Radio listeners during the process of intellectual servicing
- A word, a sound, a picture, etc. are instruments of labor in «TV Broadcasting» and «Radio Broadcasting»
- Individual and people are subjects of labor in «TV Broadcasting» and «Radio Broadcasting».

THE SOLITARY PRODUCTIVE FORCE OF THE BRANCHES OF «TV BROADCASTING» AND «RADIO BROADCASTING»

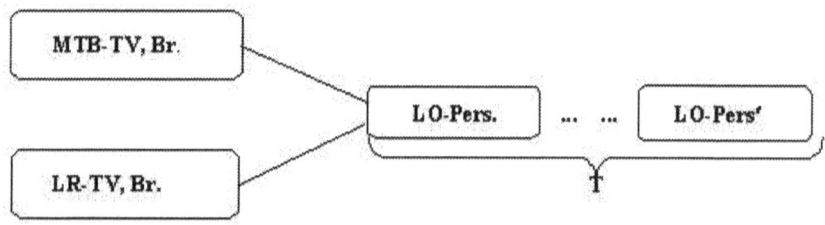

in which

MTB—TB, RB—means and instruments of «TV Broadcasting» and «Radio Broadcasting»

LR—TB, RB—labor resources of «TV Broadcasting» and «Radio Broadcasting»

SL—INDIV—subject of labor—an individual

SL—INDIV'—modified subject of labor—an individual

T—time in which the interaction of the production factors creates «enlightenment and entertainment services» of «TV Broadcasting» and «Radio Broadcasting».

The given model of «TV Broadcasting» and «Radio Broadcasting» reflects the general process that takes place in all «enlightenment and entertainment branches»: an expedient interaction between production factors, required to create «enlightenment and entertainment service». It is consumed free— S or for money—M.

The mode of interaction between the productive force factors of these two branches of intellectual production determines the character of production, distribution, exchange and consumption, of both the material-substantial terms of the «enlightenment and entertainment» activity and its immaterial results.

THE SOCIAL AIM OF «TV» AND «RADIO BROADCASTING»

According to American TV academic Mr. Nil Postman, the social aim of this branch consists of the following:

First of all, TV is a video series. We have endured a kind of evolution from printed, typographical symbols to audio-visual ones. In an average American family, the TV set works usually 8 hours a day. Thus, even by nursery school age, a child has «assimilated» some 5,000 hours TV time. So, the TV today, in its own way, reflects our culture, radically different from the pervious culture based on the printed word.

— *What do we mean by «radically»?*

— *A manuscript presents the surrounding world as an idea, like an image of an object. TV information is inert. As a rule, «Daily News» is a subject for discussion, but it does not really affect our psychological state. The small screen gives us its own interpretation of the surrounding world. The events appear and disappear on it. TV-topics last 45 seconds and change with the rhythm of commercials, as a rule. Moreover, these fragments of reality are not correlated in TV, which by nature is an art of entertainment. It turns everything into «enlightenment and entertainment»; a performance, even when it pretends to be serious. Producers of such US English is spell' programs' use the logic that if you want to gather an audience, then make a enlightenment and entertainment. Suppose you want to telecast on astrophysics? What is required for this? At minimum you should choose a proper and good-looking narrator, or a «star», pick up some «star wars» videos to supplement it and so on. As a result, all is turned into «enlightenment and entertainment».*

Nil Postman's view on the social aim of «TV» can be supplemented:

- first—the fact is that the size of the immaterial product created by «TV» and «Broadcasting» is not known
- second—the spare time of population catered for these branches is not considered a social aim;
- third—TV and Radio services are not taken into account when calculating standards of social well-being and other significant economic indicators.

THE ECONOMIC AIM OF «TV BROADCASTING» AND «RADIO BROADCASTING»

In drawing hundreds of millions of people into an intellectual service process, «TV Broadcasting» and «Radio Broadcasting» realize two purposes:

- **social**—i.e. mass production of «enlightenment and entertainment services» to utilize resource of spare time of population
- **economic**—i.e. making of maximum profits from TV Broadcasting and Radio Broadcasting.

Let's look into the matter more carefully to see how the second purpose is being realized.

In Gregory Organov's opinion, it is realized in the following manner:

«Unlike in a majority of Western countries, where TV, in one way or another is in the hands of governmental institutions, like the BBC for instance, in the US, TV has almost turned out to be under joint ownership of private and state run organizations. In practice they are unsupported by the ramified system of all-powerful commercial advertising, so in fact they sell airtime. And as soon as airtime in the US becomes the same as any other good, it brings profit in accordance to its quality. Therefore, they serve it on the American TV screen in the most rational way—«sliced» and «pre-packaged». The hardest thing to get accustomed to in the US was the method of placing American TV programs within the frames of allotted airtime.

The thing is that these programs were cut and interrupted for quite often an indefinite time. It was a well-paid business for TV corporations, since it took account of paid ads, for which payment depended on the time and kind of placement. If it was not at «prime time», but at a less advantageous time, they paid less.

A person who is not acquainted enough with the American commerce mechanism, with its scales and methods, can hardly believe the amounts of «remuneration» for commercial ads. During one of the years under examination, the expenses *of US monopolies for commercial advertising of consumer production totaled about $30 billion. The lion's share of this was spent on just TV commercials. As a matter of fact they the US mass media to «free sale» our time and frenzied profit-making, which from the principal part of future expenses on the creation of all TV shows, sports events and even information programs».[13]*

For example, the cost of the commercial was:

1) In 1975
   1 minute in daytime—$ 10,000
   1 minute at nighttime—$ 40-80,000.

2) In 1985
   1 minute during competition the final matches—$ 250-300,000.

3) In 1989
   During American football Super Cup finals
   0.5 minute—$ 645,000.

4) In 1990
   Commercial sales income of a TV network
   for one evening—1 million,
   1 minute on the CBS network—$ 150-200,000,
   The annual cost of Coca-Cola TV commercials is 120 million.[14]

The system of extracting TV profits is carried out in the following way. Let's say the NBC Company buys the rights to televise the Super Cup final from the National Football League (NFL) for $18 million. During the three-hour long transmission, the company allots 24 minutes for commercials that bring $ 31 million. If you add to this, the receipts from commercial advertisements in the course of the one-and-a-half-hour programmes preceding the Super Cup final and after its finished then you will see that the total profit is about $ 40 million. The $10 million income for NBC will be reached in the end despite taking into account the cost of the transmission itself.[15]

TV companies get such vast sums of money that they naturally spare neither strength nor resources to obtain the most popular and prestigious kind of competitions and sports events. Competitive struggle between TV compa-

---

13 «Culture» July 30, «What is TV air?» by G. Organov.

14 In 1976 cost of the transmission rights from the Montreal Olympics was 168 mln. francs. Transmitting the Olympic games from Los Angels (the ABC Channel) cost 1700 mln. francs and transmitting the Olympic games from Seoul (the ABC Channel)—2400 mln. francs.

15 Business World, Feb. 28, «Magazine of convenience», S. Gouskov.

nies has led to even more sudden leap in prices for TV transmissions. One can only imagine that over the last 20 years, the price for transmitting the Super Cup football final has increased 18 times!

The increase in the competitive struggle of TV companies helped sports leagues and associations increase their own profits. In the early 60's, TV and NFL profits, for example, made up 36% of their gross turnover. Now profits are counted billions. The NFL concluded a four-year contract with TV companies two years ago to the tune of $3.6 billion. As a result, each of the 28 teams in this League receives annually $30 million. Famous, professional baseball team the New York Yankees has signed a 12-year contract with the paid channel Madison Square Garden for $500 million.

It is hard to overestimate the significance of TV in the development of the sports business in the USA. Perhaps there is no other country where interests of these two «powers» are so closely interwoven. *«Relations between TV and sports serve as a good example of happy co-existence as they assist each other»*,—wrote famous writer J. Michner in early'70s.

Today we do not speak about survival but about sharing enormous profits. Moreover, profits from TV guarantee professional leagues a comfortable life for many years to come. In addition to that TV bosses try to own professional teams. Mergers of TV and sports businesses have taken place. Among the teams belonging to TV companies are hockey clubs such as New York Rangers, the Philadelphia Fliers; famous baseball teams, the Atlanta Braves and the California Angels, as well as basketball club the Atlanta Hawks and others.

Relationship between professional sport and US TV can be called a «marriage of convenience».[16]

THE ORGANIZATION OF TELEVISION AND RADIO BROADCASTING IN ENGLAND[17]

The British radio and television corporation (BBC) was the first to start transmitting regular public telecast in England in 1932. The branch has hovelled down a long, complex road since then. The era of multi-channeled television in Europe and the world has anwed. The personal portable aerials of satellite television can now receive transmission. The small screen's achievements are assessed and explained by researcher Robert Bell.

---

16 Magazine «England» 1990.

17 Business World, Feb. 28. «Marriage of convenience» by S. Gouskov.

Transmission in Britain developed as a public service, giving account of its work in Parliament. The two public institutions—the British radio and television corporation—the BBC and the independent television corporation (I.T.V) conform to the common principles and aims set out by Parliament. Among the requirements of TV transmission and Broadcasting are: a balanced selection of subjects and observed impartiality, reliability especially at those hours when children may be watching. The TV Transmission controls observance of these requirements and Broadcast Norm Council established by the government. It considers complaints lodged against radio and television. The BBC either prepares programmes itself or purchases from others. It owns two national channels: BBC-1 and BBC-2. The corporation transmits these programmes using their own network of transmitters. The channels are financed by subscription payments from TV set owners (a subscriber using a TV set without paying is acting illegally and pursued by the law). At present, subscription for a black and white TV-set is £ 24, for a color TV £ 71 a year. I.T.V is responsible for I.T.V. and Channel-4. However the department itself neither prepares nor purchases programmes. I.T.V. is divided into 14 regions, where programmes come from 15 independent companies (London is served by two companies). The Channel-4 telecompany transmits in England, Scotland and Northern Ireland. The Wales department of the fourth channel serves wales. Outside organizations pay I.T.V and Channel-4 to advertise their goods and services. It has become quite usual in Britain that transmitting is interrupted approximality every 20 minutes for showing advertisements.

All channels show light entertainment programs, documentary and feature films, sports at and world events. Shares of each telecast on each channel are different. BBC-1 transmits 120 hours a week and shows programs on general topics and also for children. BBC-2 (102 hours) pays more attention to different minorities (social, cultural, etc.), «education», «enlightenment» and «entertainment» foreign films. I.T.V. is a channel of general character with children's programs. It operates 24 hours a day. Channel-4 is the youngest. It is only 15 years old. It supplements I.T.V. with programs intended to satisfy not popular but narrow and special tastes. It is provided with telecasts by filmmakers and T.V program producers.

It is widely believed that British television is the best in the world. Possessing four high quality channels, Britain is in a unique position and English programmes, such as the BBC's dramatization of Oscar Wild's «The Ginger Tree» are sold all over the world. Some telecompanies in Europe simply retransmit BBC-1 and BBC-2 programs.

Public opinion polls «enlightenment and entertainment» that English people are quite content with each of the four channels. What is significant is that video recorders, in Britain, are used primarily for recording and watching telecasts at a suitable time, not for watching rented films. Moreover, a program is often recorded when a different channel is being watched.

Satisfaction with BBC and I.T.V. has suggested that cable and satellite television «Straight at home», that is to say, a television received by personal portable satellite dishes, will never be able to compete with them. In fact, satisfaction with «ordinary» television just meant a slow start for the new technology. More and more people are now installing cable television in their homes and buying satellite dishes, which are selling even faster than video recorders and microwaves at the dawn of their existence.

Cable television owners provide their consumers with extra channels, several of which belong to BBC and I.T.V. They transmit light entertainment, sports, music and, of course, socially-useful programs, compulsory by the Law.

At first cable systems were designated only to transmit teleprograms and broadcast in regions where, due to their local particularities, reception quality was low. But in 1983, the government allowed several independent cable television companies to sell their experimental service to 11 local networks. At present, after the establishment of a large number of networks, about 20 million houses found themselves in their zone. But nonetheless, in many American specialists' opinion, cable television in Britain was created over a long time. They think that it was motivated, mostly because large capacity systems have been so far limited by new city micro-districts. In rural areas, where there are few consumers, their number is insignificant. To modernize and expand these systems is more complicated in Britain than in the USA, where most power and telephone lines «stride» on posts, on which it is easier to erect a cable.

Each cable television company consists of up to thirty channels, selected by them at their discretion. As a result, intellectual consumption by the tele-audience depends on the local station. So people quite often make do with few different kinds of programs.

Sources of programs vary considerably. Some shows and films are purchased from domestic and foreign companies, others are made in the companies' own studios, in particular local news and programmes only interesting to a small group of district inhabitants. Many programs are received by satellite and re-transmitted in to subscriber's homes. At first, British and European companies, preparing programs for satellite transmission were only cable television installed. Now the tele-audience can receive a direct signal through their dishes. It is thanks to this, that one can say that pan-European television and enormous commercial opportunities of advertisement have become real.

Some experts may believe that the onset of «Straight at home» transmission portends the destruction of cable TV in Britain, but one cannot help but think that in this country, cable television, whose existence depends on two way communication, possesses a certain potential, in the field of television-bank operations, home purchases, etc. Realization of this means advertisement of goods and services on TV, ordering what one needs right away and just paying one's bank a bill. And all that can be done without getting up from the armchair at just the press of button.

After the American satellite «Telestar» was launched in the early 60's, image and sound was directed by TV stations in to the sky and then back to earth. In fact, beaming round thousands of earth transmitters. That opened direct transmission across seas and oceans. It became habitual for the British tele-audience for many programmes come directly from satellite.

It must be noted that Britain already has a strong field in creating programs for international satellite TV. About a quarter of all existing channels originated here: There are more satellite channels in Britain then in any other European country.

Since 1982, after putting the first British satellite television channel «TV Sky» into operation, England has become a base for 23 more satellite channels. They all deliver programs to cable television companies in Britain and all over Europe. They are owned by private companies and financed at the expense of advertisement, subscription payments and sponsorship. This profitable as well as prospective and prestigious business very often not invests money, interests in organizations with stable communication and mass information: newspapers, books, magazines and musical publishers as well as telecommunication companies. There is no ground for apprehensions about excessive concentration of the telebranch in one pair of hands. That is why British legislation provides articles to correct situations, which are considered by many in a democratic society, to be unhealthy.

Consequently, satellite television itself is not a new phenomenon in Britain. The latest and potentially more revolutionary medium aspect is «Straight at home» television.

The first organization with a base in Britain that entered the «Straight at home» market was the «TV Sky» company. In 1989, belonging to a Luxembourg company and controlled by «TV Sky», the «Astra» satellite began to operate four channels. Its signals are received all over Western Europe. Besides that, «TV Sky» owns 12 more, mostly non-English speaking channels. Their subscribers can watch absolutely all of their programs.

«TV Sky» has already sold 900,000 dishes with the 60-cm standard diameter. It is impossible to find a place in Britain where there are no such objects. They are attached to the walls of most private houses or high-rise buildings. The price of a «TV-Sky» dish and equipment amounts to about £ 350. One can rent it for about £ 13 a month. The other company, transmitting «straight at home» TV is BSB—British Satellite Broadcasting. It holds a license from the British government to transmit only in Britain. BSB is a consortium of companies with business interests in mass information. Unlike «TV-Sky» it has its own satellite «Marcopolo». It is interesting that the launch and organization of the consortium turned out to be the most expensive commercial enterprise in Britain, after laying the Channel tunnel. «BSB» had been making programs for cable TV before April 1990, when the «straight at home» programs began. Operations were delayed six months due to technical and other problems. Owing to that delay, «TV-Sky» company has had an enormous advantage in selling dishes.

It is difficult to predict the future of British television, but whatever it will be it is obvious that the new satellite channels and cable television networks in operation will begin to open «locks» of transmission.

CHAPTER 4

PROBLEMS OF THE «ENLIGHTENMENT AND ENTERTAINMENT» MARKETS OF WESTERN EUROPE, FRANCE AND DEVELOPING COUNTRIES

Civilized society puts the individual at the corner stone of the social conception and the multi-aspect development of a constantly expanding market of values and services. Requirements of an individual, family, or social group vary greatly in both general and specific features—material, intellectual and others. Each of these sub-systems of requirements constitutes a definite set composed of different types. These combinations have a definite structure, hierarchy and other features that determine their unity and systematic character.

The needs of an individual are implemented in several horizontal platitudes:

- a market of material values $\{m\,(t)\}$;
- a market of intellectual values $\{d\,(t)\}$;
- a market of medical services $\{Ym\,(t)\}$;
- a market of transport $(T\,(t))$;
- a market of military services $\{Yb\,(t)\}$.

A formalized record of an individual's «horizontal» needs would be as follows:

$$CPL = \begin{cases} \{m(t)\} = \{m_1(t), m_2(t), \ldots m_r(t), \ldots\} \\ \{d(t) = \{d_1(t), d_2(t), \ldots d_k(t), \ldots\} \\ Ym(t) = \{Ym_1(t), Ym_2(t), \ldots Ym_j(t), \ldots\} \\ Tp(t) = \{Tp_1(t), Tp_2(t), \ldots Tp_n(t), \ldots\} \\ Yb(t) = \{Yb_1(t), Yb_2(t), \ldots Yb_h(t), \ldots\} \end{cases}$$

in which

СПЛ—system of an individual's needs implemented in a market of material values {m (t)}, intellectual {d (t)}, medical services {Ym (t)}, services of transport;

{Tp (t)}-military services {Yb (t)};

t—parameter revealing a mutability of these relations in time;

{m(t)}—system of an individual's material needs constitutes a variety of vectors of these specific requirements.

A system of an individual's needs looks graphically as follows:

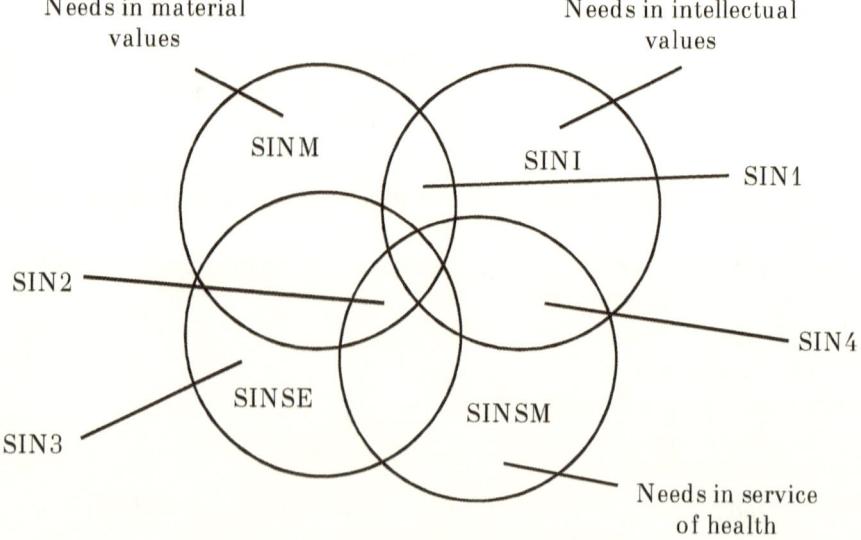

Needs in material values

Needs in intellectual values

SINM

SINI

SIN1

SIN2

SIN4

SINSE

SINSM

SIN3

Needs in service of health

Above picture reveals a variety of consumption relations of an individual in a «pure» kind, i.e. only in the market of material values, intellectual services, public health sphere services and services in a scientific and military sphere.

THE INTELLECTUAL PRODUCTION

The branches of intellectual production create their own specific market that consists of the intellectual values and services. In terms of the commodity relations they come out as a product of labor, supposedly to be exchanged by means of sale-purchase. These values and services possess the following properties:
- A property to meet an intellectual need (both personal and production ones);
- A property to be exchanged for other values and services.

The intellectual values (books, pictures, films) coming out in material form and the intellectual services of a teacher, singer, dancer and priest are created by concrete labor:
-the labor of a writer is embodied in a book;
-the labor of a composer is embodied in the notes of music at a concert;
-the labor of a teacher in chemistry or physics is embodied in a teacher's service;
-the labor of a musician is embodied in a musician.

Now we should consider the portion of this specific market, which is formed by «the enlightenment and entertainment branches», out of all the aggregate intellectual values and services: «Culture», «Art», «Sports-entertainment», «Cinema», «Religion», «TV Broadcasting» and «Radio Broadcasting».
A development of «enlightenment and entertainment branches» has its own specific counting point both in the production of «enlightenment and entertainment services» and in the field of their consumption. For instance, 100 years ago «a major landmark» for «enlightenment and entertainment branches» was the year when cinema was born—1895. Economically developed countries had this approximate correlation of «enlightenment and entertainment services» in the market that year:

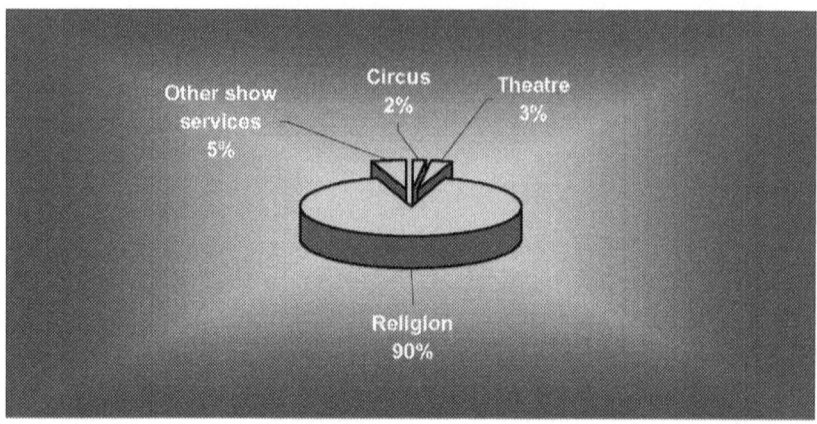

The first cinema film was shown in Paris on 28th December 1895, with nearly 40 people present. Within two days, thousands people wished to watch the cinema «enlightenment and entertainment». From that day on «film distribution» developed very quickly. Its output increased 1000 times during the first years. Thus, for instance, George Melee, a Frenchman, (owner of the company «Star Films») shot 4000 short films between 1896 and 1914, and the other film companies did not fall behind. 28th December 1895 is the date when a technical revolution started in «enlightenment and entertainment branches». An era of electrical and mechanical production of the «enlightenment and entertainment services» started on that day. This event can be compared to the significance of invention of the steam engine for production, which replaced hard labor and increased labor productivity by hundreds of thousand of times.

The second counting point for «enlightenment and entertainment branches» is 7th, May, 1905. The first radio transmission took place on this day. The radio era started. Economically developed countries had the following correlation of «enlightenment and entertainment services» in that year:

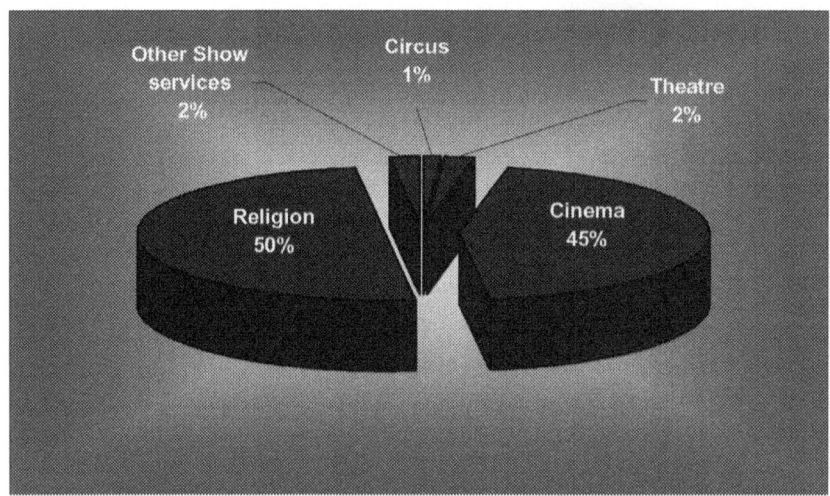

Within several years «radio services» occupied a considerable place in the market of «enlightenment and entertainment services».

1912 is believed to be <u>the third counting point</u>. It is the year Hollywood, a factory of cinema production, was founded. «Enlightenment and entertainment» market of developed countries was that year approximately as follows:

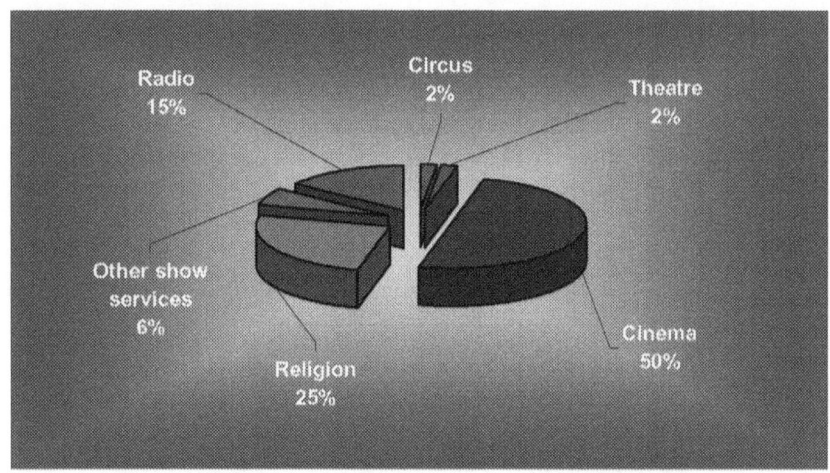

1927 can be seen as the fourth counting point when sound was invented in the cinema. Sound brought a «new breath» into cinema art and considerably expanded its borders. The Golden age of Hollywood started and nearly 7,500 full films were produced in its studios between 1930 and 1945.

The invention of the TV set is the fifth counting point.[18]

The expansion of TV has changed the structure of «enlightenment and entertainment services» consumed over the last 40 years, by considerably narrowing the borders of the STP resource assimilated by the theatre, circuses, concerts and cinema. It is easy to see this while analyzing the statistics of the branches, on the one hand, and while analyzing the expanding borders of TV and Radio Broadcasting assimilation, on the other hand.

Despite a decrease in the volumes of cinema assimilating the spare time resource, it still occupies one of the leading places in the intellectual sphere of social production.

A close interaction between the branches of «Art» and «TV Broadcasting» occurred in the economically developed countries in the mid 1970s. Their relation to a great extent has a competitive angle. «*In the developed countries where an antagonism between cinema production and TV broadcasting is an open struggle of two screens…, a competitive war of two branches of the audio and video business. And, sometimes taking rather strange forms when the opponents find some unexpected interest in the final defeat of each other, this strange war ends most frequently with a mutually beneficial financial partnership…Cinema production and TV Broadcasting cannot exist without each other, both in the sphere of production and in the sphere of distribution… Such regularity is seen more and more clearly with the passing of time…in the joining of film production and TV programs in common organizational frames*».[19]

Andriash Sekphyu makes the following conclusions in his article «On the new place of cinema in the structure of communications»:

1. «*The future of film as film distribution is to be considered within the system of film-TV broadcasting only—cinema halls.*

2. *This supposes a conscious usage of the distribution capabilities of a traditional cinema hall, a cinema club, social distribution and TV broadcasting.*

---

18 The invention of satellite communication can be seen as the sixth counting point, etc.

19 See the book «Massive Communications», p.98.

3. *The new structure must solve the contradictions that occur due to low effectiveness in utilizing material and the intellectual means spent on creating cinemas and TV films.*

4. *The new structure must be based on (together with pure quantitative criteria) qualitative indices that exclude a fetish for audience numbers, which is characteristic of the present period».*

The structure of producing intellectual services proposed by A. Sekphyu can include other structures such as «theatre spectacle-TV Broadcasting». Each of them must have an economic base and the advantages of the organization of one structure over another must be proved.

WESTERN EUROPE «ENLIGHTENMENT AND ENTERTAINMENT» MARKET TRENDS[20]

These days more and more figures in West European art think it necessary to rebuff the onslaught of American mass culture. This fight has been fought most fiercely in fields such as cinema and television—the major channels of distribution of USA «intellectual production». Already 60 per cent of the films shown in Germany are of Hollywood origin. French and domestic films make up the remainder in approximately equal proportions. 80 per cent of the films shown in Great Britain are American.

The main reason for this situation is the fact that Hollywood commands much greater funds than West European studios. Cinema theatres of the Old World are overwhelmed with a wave of films stuffed with all kinds of thinkable and unimagible special effects that one could only invent. Vast amounts of money are needed to create them.

Cinematography is not the only sphere of intellectual culture in which Americans can celebrate their victory over (Western) Europe. West European television is saturated with American production companies, which makes, on average, about 70 per cent of the total volume of telecasts. The US attack on culture will be very difficult to contain as satellite and cable television spreads. Having a vast home market, US TV companies cover all the expenses of film production and entertainment programs, then sell them at deliberately knock-down prices in Western Europe, getting their profit, and at the same time completely ruining their West European competitors. For example, the infamous TV series «Dallas» cost only 25,000 dollars to show most West

20 Weekly magazine «Abroad» No.11

European countries. France decided to produce their own analogue of this TV series, at a cost of 200,000 per film.

Although Hollywood produces less than 10% of the world's motion pictures the USA exports one third of the world's films, reaping more than 50 per cent of all film distribution profits. Under such circumstances the anxiety of West Europeans is quite understandable. Counteraction measures proposed by many cultural figures and representatives of the cinema industry are diametrically opposed to one another.

The first measure is the creation of cinema works that satisfy national interests and the traditions of each West European country. Production of «local» films does not require great expense and takes the distinctions of each country into account.

The second counter measure is refusal to orient to give «national a supra» character to European cinema production, as well as the film towards their own country's spectators. A new generation of West European film producers are calling for films to be cash successful.

Artists in different countries are called on to make «profitable» Euro hits. Representatives of a new generation favor attracting private capital investors, while demanding the decisive artistic say for themselves to solve all these questions. A commercial success is considered of paramount importance.

The idea to create supra-national films was apprehended by many West European creative film figures as a *«betrayal of the national culture»*. Their protests are also supported by certain political circles who consider that such an approach *«might lead to the intellectual colonization of Western Europe»*.

A. PROBLEMS OF THE «ENLIGHTENMENT AND ENTERTAINMENT» MARKET IN FRANCE

Pierre Biyar published his article «Cinema on the brink of a precipice» in the Parisian weekly «Poyanne». In his article he analyzed the interaction and interdependence of film distribution and TV Broadcasting. The name of the article alone passes judgment about the state and conditions that this branch of the intellectual production has come to.

Nowadays the heads of film distribution are worried about the situation. The same tendencies occur in all countries with multi-channel and 24 hours. At the same time it is obvious that the difficult relations between cinema production and TV Broadcasting is aggravated by the West, mostly due to apparent commercial logic.

The cultural sphere of France has come through great and rapid changes resulting in deadlock.[21] France entered into the TV era in the 1950s. By the 1960s the number of TV sets had reached 10 million. But at same time, the number of cinema visitors dropped distinctly from 435 million to 175 million visits per annum. It was the first TV blow to cinematography. Cinema managed to adapt itself to the situation: between 1970-1985, cinema attendance was steady (170-185 million per annum) while the number of TV sets in family homes grew to 18 million. It seems that cinematography firmly consolidated its sphere of influence. Then all of a sudden, Frenchmen had to deal with six commercial TV channels instead of three state TV programs, which had been under strict control, with slack competition between them. Those six new channels played by more flexible rules and used the confusion characteristic of the initial stage of development, to win audiences. It was the second TV strike against cinematography. However, that strike did not touch all existing cinematography structures. New markets, new financial sources opened for film makers (producers, directors, script writers etc.) but at the same time they were risking, one way or another, the loss of their creative individuality. In addition, the future prospects of film distributors (the whole film distribution system) have narrowed, so much so that they may disappear altogether under super cruel conditions of competition.

At present over 1300 different films are shown on TV annually. There are some evenings when each of the six channels shows a film at the same time. It is a miracle that there are still several million French people who turn their backs on such variety of shows at home, have their houses to pay to see a film at a cinema. The tragedy is that such people are becoming fewer and fewer.

The film distribution owners showed a rare unanimity at their meeting in Paris. They blamed the government for being oblivious of the traditional policy of defending the interests of national cinema, they threatened to take the TV companies to Court and voted to introduce a system of financial punishments. They demanded a lot, but very few in Government heard them.

On the other hand, the struggle made by the film distributors were considerably weakened by a wide spread conviction that declining attendance cannot be avoided. Thus, it is necessary that a number of cinemas up and down the country conform to the new conditions. But here lies the very problem and the very danger. The experience of other countries shows that while

---

21 Weekly magazine «Abroad» No.4 (137), p.22 «Cinema on the verge of disaster»

cinemas give up ground to TV, they then regain their position and audience, provided the audience's interest does not fall below a certain point, from which it is not possible to climb back.

With the advanced US TV network in 1965, cinema attendance was about 1.2 billion. It then fell to 720 million, but in 1986 it bounced back to 1.1 billion. If we count how many times a resident of one country or another goes to the cinema a year, the average American went about six times a year until 1960, three times in the 1970s and about five times a year today. 20 years ago, Italians and Germans went to the cinema 10 times a year, but now they only go twice a year. In Great Britain the index is equal to 1.2 visits without growth, although 30 years ago an average British citizen visited the cinema nine times yearly. A Frenchman also went 9 times a year in the 1950s, but only 3.5 times in the 1970s when France suffered TV shock for the first time. In 1987, a Frenchman went to the cinema 2.5 times a year. Fortunately this index did not fall below the number 2 as a result of the second shock. Otherwise the whole national film production would have been seriously compromised and unable to recover, as in Great Britain when it provoked mass cinema shutdowns.

Moreover, cinema has to meet new demands from an audience that wants something that TV does not give, i.e. a large screen, excellent quality of sound and picture—a perfect, special show. The «Homon» Company has a new large screen and Dolby stereo system in all its cinemas. The 24-metre screen at the «Film Panorama» cinema attracted a considerable number of people.

As we can see, film distributors have to modernize quickly in order to survive structural problem connected to heavy competition from TV.

B. THE MODERN «ENLIGHTENMENT AND ENTERTAINMENT» MARKET SITUATION IN DEVELOPING COUNTRIES

Egypt is the country of youth.22 More than 60 per cent of their population is thirty years old or younger. Secondly, the youth sector of the population has very moderate means. That is why most young men spend their spare time in the streets and, if they are lucky enough to scrape a pound or two together, they run eagerly to the cinema. Statistical data shows that mod-

---

22 «Abroad» Weekly, No.12

ern American action pictures are more popular than others. Action-packed Egyptian films are also quite popular, but not so much. Serious works of art, in which critical social problems are raised, just disappear from screens after two or three days.

The film market in ARE is in private hands. Each proprietor tries to buy a film at the cheapest price possible and get the most profit from each «enlightenment and entertainment». Strangely enough the cheapest films in the market are American primitive adventure pictures. They cost Egyptian cinema owners two or three times less than West European films and 5-10 times less than a good American film.

The second reason is psychological. Smart Hollywood dealers have to determine exactly what the unassuming spectator would like to see. Supermen and superwomen, martial arts and space wars, fists of steel and rapid-firing pistols—all these and many more are compulsory components, usually combined with an elementary, but dynamic plot.

Television, unlike cinematography is a state-run organization. Judging by the figures, American show business has settled down solidly even here. Three Egyptian TV channels show nearly 20 American pictures and TV films, as well as numerous cartoons, commercials and music programs weekly, yet only 15-16 Arabic films—confirmed by official state statistics. Uncle Sam's presence on local TV screen is very impressive.

But Egyptian art is still trying, although with almost no success, to resist American show business. But Americans have achieved absolute, unconditional victory in the field of the video.

As you can see, American culture dominates all three possible screens: cinema, television and video.

Fikhri Salekh, Deputy Culture Minister of Egypt, was categorical:

- Predominance of American cinema production on our screens is not conditioned by a cultural policy of the Egyptian government. On the contrary, we would like our population to have a chance to get to know arts from different countries and nations. But unfortunately businessmen often indulge the low requirements of spectators and are led by profit hunting. Increasing the quality of taste is a matter of national importance. To this end, we are now attaching great importance to the role our national artists can play.

And what do the most progressive figures of Egyptian culture think of American dominance?

Film director Yusef Shakhin noted on the matter that: «It is an occupation! Indeed it is a real «cultural occupation»! Are you out of your mind to bring

4000 cassettes from the USA with ungifted films to show this garbage to the audience?»

«Cinematography has not created even 400 decent films during its whole history. But businessmen are careless about the quality of pictures and ideology that they bring. The businessmen are only interested in money and the profits they can gain. But Egypt is a freedom-loving nation. They got rid of their king and threw the colonizers out of the country. All occupiers were defeated. But what is going on now is something new. Again we are experiencing occupation though not many people feel it». The director went on: «What the American film business is doing now may be regarded as a crime against culture. Of course, you understand that I am speaking about cheap things».

CHAPTER 5

TIME BUDGET OF PEOPLE AS A SYSTEM OF SOCIAL INDICATORS

I propose to use a time budget of people, its proportion and structure as a system of indicators. Any individual or group, both in producing values and services, as in consuming them, possess a temporary projection that is expressed in every day expenses in time. They just make a system of indices that reflect a personified geography of relations during a day, week, month, quarter, six months and a year. Time and man are the indivisible or prime concepts.

Indeed, the time budget reflects an interlacing of various factors, moments and tendencies—phenomena of social life. The time budget of people can be called a mirror of social change. This is the mirror, which to a great extend adequately reflects all the contradictions of the social phenomena and the qualitative jumps that take place within society.

The closer we approach the mirror and in the greater the details with which we consider the social changes, the more precise is their reflection in the time budget of people, and vice versa. The less thorough the investigation, the further we stand away from it and the more vague a phenomenon becomes. The time budget of people constitutes the system of characteristics that fixes the precise border lines of formation, conception and fading away of these or those social processes.

What do the Belgians do, coming home from work, getting tired in the underground stations or in traffic jams?[23] How do they spend their spare time (the time is spare when we do not sleep, do not shop and do not work)? If a man

---

23 «In captivity of TV», Beatrice Delve, «Abroad», 10th December.

goes to bed not later than mid night, his average spare time is five hours a day. If we are to be precise and use on the questionnaires as a basis, the spare time of a workingwoman comes to 321 minutes and the spare time of a housewife comes to 334 minutes. The men possess a little less spare time (depending on whether his wife is busy at work or is a housewife), so that it comes to 304 and 308 minutes respectively. And how do the Belgians use these hours between their work and sleep?

We shall start with men. We should admit that they try their best to maximize their hours, to get the best that life can give. They rest, they put their legs on the table, they sit in front of the TV or they enjoy themselves with their friends. In short, they do their own thing. They spend 66-71 per cent of their spare time like this. Must a man, whose wife is busy around the house all day long, help her a little? Surely he must. He spends 11 minutes on household chores whereas a husband of a workingwoman spends 22 minutes on these tasks. And how does it go for the women? They cannot spend even half of their spare time resting (a woman that does not work possesses 154 minutes for this and a woman that works possesses 149 minutes). Dishwashing, house cleaning and washing clothes laundering ruthlessly «drains her reservoir for entertainment».

Now you can ask what attention is given to children. The data from the questionnaires shame the Belgians. Nobody gives more than 16 per cent of their spare time to their sons and daughters. A terrifying statistic if we compare it to the amount of time spent watching TV. A husband of a woman who does not work spends 4 per cent of his spare time with his children and 42 per cent on TV. A husband of a workingwoman spends 7 per cent of his spare time with his children and 34 per cent watching TV. Women who do not work pay more attention to their children. They spend 16 per cent of their spare time on their children, leaving 32 per cent for TV. Workingwomen spend 10 per cent and 25 per cent respectively. What else is left? Going to friends and receiving guests takes an average of 30 minutes. Reading—15 minutes for men and 10 for women. Sports take 4 and 2 minutes respectively. Listening to the radio takes not more than 1-2 minutes. These are the figures. They do not account for differences in level of education, social class and profession. The figures are average. But you should admit that they are very expressive!

Now we consider a family again, at some time before mid night. The children have already gone to bed, dinner is over and the irritation over to washing the dishes has vanished. Now it is finally possible to de-stress. The Belgians hurry to their TV sets. The men spend 1 hour 43 minutes watching TV every day; their wives, 1 hour and 20 minutes.

The above figures and data reveal that a time budget of people is not a thought up system of indices. This is a natural system of indices. There is no alternative system of characteristics of the time budget of people that fully reflects our every day life.

The time budget of people consists of the following blocks:
1) a budget of working time;
2) a budget of time out of work, including:
   - time expenditure of a physiological character;
   - self-servicing time expenditures;
   - travel time expenditures;
3) a budget of people's spare time.

The blocks (time proportions) are closely inter-connected. An alteration in the dimensions of one of them can make compounds appear or disappear in the considered budget. Thus, a change in the length of the working day directly tells on the borders of out-of-work and people's spare time, as well as on the structure of each time block. For example, an expansion of the material and technical basis of consumer service institutions reduces the absolute dimensions of people's out-of-work time budget. An expansion of volume of the transport services also reduces the out-of-work time budget of people, on the one hand, and increases the borders of their spare time, on the other. And vice versa, due to the reduction in the material and technical basis of the consumer service institutions (due to its physical age), the out-of-work time budget will naturally increase at the expense of the reduction in people's spare time budget.

A. LIFESTYLE AS A RELATIVE SYSTEM OF SOCIAL INDICATORS

The concept of «Lifestyle» is often used in economic publications. However, until recently the internal structure of this concept has been considered, though it is closely connected.

The basic problem is to determine how and according to which characteristics any aspect of people's daily lives or various kinds of activities must be described. They must not be reflected in a non-existing system of complex indicators but in clear natural indicators.[24]

---

24 Considering the economic category of «lifestyle» we proceed from the fact that the essence of this category is to regularly repeats actions of production, distribution, exchange and consumption of material and intellectual benefits and services.

I propose to use the population time budget as a system of indicators because only through this we get a complete recording of all social processes. It uses open opportunities for further research into various kinds of human activities:
-working life
-domestic life
-spare time.

Each of these kinds of «lifestyle» is recorded in the population's time budget.

Average duration of activities;

$$Sfp = \frac{\textit{Total expenses in an investigated aggregate Period of activities}}{\textit{Investigated aggregate of periods that has these kind of expenses in a time budget}}.$$

This relatively simple indicator opens an opportunity to work out a system of new indicators of an individual's «lifestyle» from a social group. The essence of the latter lies in a formalized description of various kinds of human activities (pastime) in concrete, understandable to everyone—indicators that reflect the special features of this or that process as well as their interconnection.

I propose to consider «lifestyle» in every relatively autonomous sphere of the national economy: in material and intellectual production, in health protection, the military, and the managerial sphere. Below are the dialectic schemes of each kind of lifestyle sphere.

A general, formalized record of lifestyle appears as follows:

$$L = \frac{\sum\limits_{j=1}^{m} \sum\limits_{i=1}^{n} \sum\limits_{k=1}^{l} T_{kij}}{k \cdot m \cdot l},$$

where T_{kij} is actual duration of i-kind of activities of k-person on j-day of the
year, i.e. i=1, 2,..., n—number and scale of activities during one year, by a
portion of the k-group of the population.

This system of indicators is an average statistical characteristic of an individual's family or a social group. For each social group of the population, these
indicators are a generalized system of characteristics that determine their
lifestyle.

The «lifestyle» category as a whole unites in itself particular aspects, namely:
  -material;
  -intellectual;
  -domestic and others.

Each of them expressed an appropriate system of characteristics of the population's time budget to describe changes, formed lines, vectors and value
orientation of both an individual and a social group. They reflect an interconnected totality of contradictions, give opportunities for estimating
directions and change rates in certain social processes.

DIALECTIC SHEME OF WORKER LIFESTYLE (MATERIAL PRODUCTION)[25]

	Dialectic structure of working lifestyle of those participating in material production (MP)*	Dialectic structure of domestic lifestyle of those participating in material production (MP)**	Dialectic structure of spare time lifestyle of those participating in material production (MP)***
Thesis	Working lifestyle of those participating in division I MP	Domestic lifestyle of those participating in division I MP	Spare time lifestyle of those participating in division I MP
Antithesis	Working lifestyle of those participating in division II MP	Domestic lifestyle of those participating in division II MP	Spare time lifestyle of those participating in division II MP
Synthesis	Aggregate working lifestyle of those participating in divisions I and II MP	Aggregate domestic lifestyle of those participating in divisions I and II MP	Aggregate spare time off lifestyle of those participating in divisions I and II MP

*   Working time budget is taken as a basis.
**   Spare time budget is taken as a basis.
*** Spare time budget is taken as a basis.

25 Considering this dialectic scheme we proceed from the fact that material production consists of two interconnected divisions:
-Division I MP—branches producing means of production, equipment etc.;
-Division II—branches producing consumer goods.

DIALECTIC SHEME OF WORKER LIFESTYLE (INTELLECTUAL PRODUCTION)[26]

	Dialectic structure of working lifestyle of those participating in intellectual production (IP)[*]	Dialectic structure of domestic life of those participating in intellectual production (IP)[**]	Dialectic structure free time lifestyle of those participating in intellectual production (IP)[***]
Thesis	Working lifestyle of those participating in division I IP	Domestic lifestyle of those participating in division I IP	Spare time lifestyle of those participating in division I IP
Antithesis	Working lifestyle of those participating in division II IP	Domestic lifestyle of those participating in division II IP	Spare time lifestyle of those participating in division II IP
Synthesis	Aggregate working lifestyle of those participating in divisions I and II IP	Aggregate domestic lifestyle of those participating in divisions I and II IP	Aggregate spare time lifestyle of those participating in divisions I and II IP

*   Working time budget is taken as a basis.
**   Spare time budget is taken as a basis.
*** Spare time budget is taken as a basis.

---

26 Constructing this dialectic scheme of worker lifestyle intellectual production I proceeded from the fact that it consists of two divisions:

-Division I IP—branches producing material intellectual benefits: books, pictures, films, etc.;

-Division II IP—branches producing services: «Education», «Enlightenment and entertainment branches».

DIALECTIC SHEME OF WORKER LIFESTYLE (HEALTH PROTECTION SPHERE)[27]

	Dialectic structure of working lifestyle of those participating in the health protection sphere (HPS)	Dialectic structure of domestic life of those participating in the health protection sphere (HPS)	Dialectic structure of time off lifestyle of those participating in the health protection sphere (HPS)
Thesis	Working lifestyle of those participating in division I HPS	Domestic lifestyle of those participating in division I HPS	Spare time lifestyle of those participating in division I HPS
Antithesis	Working lifestyle of those participating in division II HPS	Domestic lifestyle of those participating in division II HPS	Spare time lifestyle of those participating in division II HPS
Synthesis	Aggregate working lifestyle of those participating in divisions I and II HPS	Aggregate domestic lifestyle of those participating in divisions I and II HPS	Aggregate spare time lifestyle of those participating in divisions I and II HPS

---

27 Constructing this dialectic scheme of worker lifestyle health protection sphere I proceeded from the fact that is consists of two interconnected divisions:

◊ Division I of health protection includes: branches producing medical, preparations as well as medical equipment;

◊ Division II of health sphere includes: branches, rendering medical services, using medical equipment, medicine and preparations made in the division I of the health protection sphere.

DIALECTIC SHEME OF WORKER LIFESTYLE (MANAGEMENT SPHERE)[28]

	Dialectic structure of working lifestyle of those participating in the health protection sphere (MS)	Dialectic structure of domestic life of those participating in the health protection sphere (MS)	Dialectic structure of time off lifestyle of those participating in the health protection sphere (MS)
Thesis	Working lifestyle of those participating in division I MS	Domestic lifestyle of those participating in division I MS	Spare time lifestyle of those participating in division I MS
Antithesis	Working lifestyle of those participating in division II MS	Domestic lifestyle of those participating in division II MS	Spare time lifestyle of those participating in division II MS
Synthesis	Aggregate working lifestyle of those participating in divisions I and II MS	Aggregate domestic lifestyle of those participating in divisions I and II MS	Aggregate spare time lifestyle of those participating in divisions I and II MS

---

28 Constructing this dialectic scheme of the worker lifestyle management sphere, I proceeded from the fact that it consists of two inter connected divisions:

◊ Division I of the management sphere—branches producing technical means of management, account etc.;

◊ Division II of the management sphere—workers rendering management services, using technical means of management made in division I of management.

The essence of these criteria must be the total sum of the absolute expenses of people's time on i-article in a people's time budget of a region, city and locality on one hand, and of the expenses of past, direct and aggregate labor on the other hand.

$$\text{Criterion ``A''} = \frac{\sum\limits_{i=1}^{n} PTB_i}{\sum\limits_{j=1}^{m} EPL_{ij}} \rightarrow \max$$

$$\text{Criterion ``B''} = \frac{\sum\limits_{i=1}^{n} PTB_i}{\sum\limits_{j=1}^{m} ELL_{ij}} \rightarrow \max$$

$$\text{Criterion ``C''} = \frac{\sum\limits_{i=1}^{n} PTB_i}{\sum\limits_{j=1}^{m} ECL_{ij}} \rightarrow \max$$

where

PTB—people's time budget;

PTB_i—absolute amount of i-in a time budget of a researched group of people;

n—size of researched group;

EPL_{ij}, ELL_{ij}, ECL_{ij}—expenses of past, living and collective labor of j—institution enterprise developing time budget of i—group of population.

DIALECTIC STRUCTURE
OF RELATIVE CRITERIA FOR PEOPLE'S TIME BUDGET

Criteria thesis «A» $= \dfrac{\sum\limits_{j=1}^{m}\sum\limits_{i=1}^{n} PTB_{ij}}{\sum\limits_{j=1}^{m}\sum\limits_{j=1}^{m} EPL_{ij}}$

Criteria antithesis «B» $= \dfrac{\sum\limits_{j=1}^{m}\sum\limits_{i=1}^{n} PTB_{ij}}{\sum\limits_{j=1}^{m}\sum\limits_{j=1}^{m} ELL_{Tij}}$

Criteria synthesis «C» $= \dfrac{\sum\limits_{j=1}^{m}\sum\limits_{i=1}^{n} PTB_{ij}}{\sum\limits_{j=1}^{m}\sum\limits_{j=1}^{m} ECL_{ij}}$

---

where PTB $_{ij}$—i-article in the population's time budget (absolute size of i-item in j-group of population's budget).

The proposed criteria system may be complemented if necessary to reduce the amount of irrational time expenses or widen the borders of the i-item in a population's time budget. Then the complemented criterion of investments in using the population's time budget (Δ PTB) could be written as follows:[29]

---

29 In criteria «A», «B», «C», the other parts of the population's time budget can be used instead PTB to use its components:
- PWTB—population's working time budget;
- PTOB—population's spare time budget;
- PSTB—population sphere spare budget.

$$
\begin{cases}
\textbf{Thesis} & = \dfrac{\sum\limits_{i=1}^{n}\left|\Delta PTB_i\right|}{\sum\limits_{j=1}^{m}\Delta EPL\,j} \rightarrow \max \\[3em]
\textbf{Antithesis} & = \dfrac{\sum\limits_{i=1}^{n}\left|\Delta PTB_i\right|}{\sum\limits_{j=1}^{m}\Delta ELL\,j} \rightarrow \max \\[3em]
\textbf{Synthesis} & = \dfrac{\sum\limits_{i=1}^{n}\left|\Delta PTB_i\right|}{\sum\limits_{j=1}^{m}\Delta ECL\,j} \rightarrow \max
\end{cases}
$$

One should note that employment expenses are equal to the expenses of developing the «space» of the population's working time in material, intellectual, health, military, and managerial sphere.

TIME BUDGET OF PEOPLE AND PARTICIPATION OF THE SERVICE BRANCHES IN ITS FORMATION
(in average as per capita)

Types of time expenses	Minutes a week	Participation of the service branches in forming the time budget	Minutes a week
Regulated time	1482.4		
I. Working time and the time expenses connected to work	1039.0		
		I. Time of consuming the services by people, the regulated time	489.4
including: working time	864.0	Including that per branch:	
The time expenses connected to traveling to work and back, preparation of the working place, etc.	175.0	Public catering	46.0
		Education	443.4
II. Educational time and the time expenses connected to education	443.4		
including: Auditorium and out-of-auditorium classes	395.9		
Time expenses connected to education (traveling to the place of study, preparation for the classes, etc.)	46.5		
Non-regulated time	8597.6		
III. Time of labor in household work including:	1097.8	II. Time of consuming the services by people within household work including	166.65
Shopping	152.0	including	
Household work (laundering, repair and manufacture of some items, etc.)	258.0	As per the branches:	

		Trade	152.0
		Consumer services	10.8
Cleaning	84.3	Housing and common facilities	1.25
Water delivery, heating, repair of the common facilities, yard cleaning	110.0	communication	2.6
Dish washing, cooking	341.5		
Child care	130.2		
Visiting post-office, bank, etc.	2.6		
Visiting enterprises of consumer services	10.8		
Consumption of consumer services given by private persons	8.4		
IV. Time of labor in personal subsidiary farms	171.6	Total: time of consuming the services within the limits of labor activities	656.06
Total: non-production labor activities (III + IV)	1269.4		
Total: complete labor loading (I + II + III + IV)	2751.8		
V. Meeting physiological Needs	4855.8		
Including:			
Eating	447.2		
Sleep	4038.0	III. Time of consuming services meeting their physiological needs as per the branches of:	123.6
Personal hygiene	240.0	Public health, physical culture, social provision	100.6
Medical treatment	130.6	Public catering	9.2
		Consumer servicing of people	13.8
VI. Spare time	2472.3	IV. Time of consuming the	

1. Cultural way of spending time including:	361.8	services during people's spare time as per the branches:	323.7
reading a newspaper	54.0		
reading fiction	155.4		
Shows	55.8	Education	58.9
Amateur and art classes at home, in clubs and study groups	96.6	Culture and art, public health, physical culture and social provision	79.7
2. Postal tuition and social work	58.5	Public catering	5.7
Including:		Communication	5.4
Postal tuition	15.9		
Social work	42.6		
3. Active rest	338.8		
Including:			
Physical training and sports	73.6		
Tourism	0.7		
Socially arranged rest in the country (guest-houses, holiday hotels, bases for tourism)	30.5		
Walking, hunting, fishing, staying in the country to rest	234.0		
4. Passive rest	887.7		
Including:			
Watching TV	48.0		
Listening to the radio	72.0		
Visiting cafes and restaurants	5.7		
Talking to relatives and friends in the street, at home and by telephone	90.0		
Inactive rest	462.0		
Receiving and visiting guests	210.0		
5. Busy with children, children in the kinder-garden and at day nurseries	151.7		
Including:			
Busy with children	108.7		
Children in kinder-gardens and day nurseries	43.0		

6. The spare time spent on «other» (other occupation)	673.8	Passenger's transport	174.0
Total:	10080.0	Total time of con-suming the services	1277.35

CHAPTER 6

POTENTIAL BORDERS OF THE «ENLIGHTENMENT AND ENTERTAINMENT» MARKET

The time estimations are the determining ones in the intellectual sphere while calculating the «supply and demand» function as a phase of «producing» intellectual services, which coincides with the phase of their «consumption» in time. In this way the time budget of people is the instrument that assists an investigation of «enlightenment and entertainment services», to establish its absolute borders in city, region and country.

The market parameters depend on a number of factors:

- first, on the number of inhabiting people. For example, if five hours is the average amount of spare time per capita, the potential spare time of 100,000 people is 500,000 hours a day. The potential resource of 200,000 people comes to 1 billion hours a day and 365 billion hours per annum;

- second, the social demographic structure of the population. For instance, if workers live mostly in a district, their potential spare time resource is considerably less than that if a district where the majority of inhabitants are students and retired people;

- third, the infrastructure of material, intellectual and other spheres of social production. In places with developed infrastructure the dimensions of the potential resource STP (potential borders of the «enlightenment and entertainment» market) are considerably bigger than they are in places where there are no pre-school institutions for children, where people spend most of their time in queues and where public transport is inefficient. The time expenses increase in these areas.

A rational utilization of the components of out-of-work time is a factor that increases potential borders of the «enlightenment and entertainment» market. It means reducing the so-called irrational expenses connected with household work and self-servicing to a minimum. These and other factors are considered necessary while determining the potential borders of the «enlightenment and entertainment» market of a town, region and country.

A. CALCULATION OF THE POTENTIAL BORDERS OF THE «ENLIGHTENMENT AND ENTERTAINMENT» MARKET

An analysis of the sociological data confirms that a structure of man's spare time and its absolute dimensions depend on the character and content of labor, social and personal life and demographic factors of sex, age, education and salary, etc. The factors establish the borders for the potential resource of people's spare time—of the potential borders for the «enlightenment and entertainment» market.

A topical consideration of the problems of the «enlightenment and entertainment» market is conditioned by the absolute values of the spare time resource of people (STP). For instance, engineers and technical officers have an annual spare time resource of 1900 hours, while laborers have 1700 hours. The annual spare time resource per capita comes is an average of 1800 hours. While knowing the data and size of the working population, it is possible to calculate the borders of the «enlightenment and entertainment» market at the first approach:

141.9 million people x 1800 = 255.42 billion men-hours.

The volume of spare time for people who do not work (children and housewives) comes to:

86.0 million people[30] x 10 hours x 365 days= 313.9 billion men-hours,

50.5 million retired people have a spare time of:

50.5 million people x 10 hours x 365 days = 184.3 billion men-hours.

---

30 This group of the people (including children) has a spare time of 10 hours a day, the rest of time is spent on physiological needs—sleeping, eating, etc.

The potential borders of the «enlightenment and entertainment» market segment for 8.23 million students is calculated as follows:

8.23 million people x 10 hours x 365 days = 30.3 billion men-hours.

The total spare time accumulated by all segments of the «enlightenment and entertainment» market, as given above, is 784 billion hours.

It should also be noted that the «enlightenment and entertainment» market could be considered on the other planes as well: there is one segment structure of this specific market in the context of age and another in the context of education, etc.

B. POTENTIAL BORDERS OF THE «ENLIGHTENMENT AND ENTERTAINMENT» MARKET IN THE CONTEXT OF THE RELATIVELY AUTONOMOUS SPHERES OF PRODUCTION

I believe the methodology of such investigations requires a considerable elaboration of the context of common logic. It is principally as follows: the time budget of people is to be investigated, both in the context of the different branches and according to the separate spheres of social production (material, intellectual, public health, administration and others). Each of the spheres has its own specific budget of time (work time, out-of-work time and spare time) that is peculiar of this particular sphere. Thus, if we proceed the material production (MP) consists of two divisions (production of the means production is Division I of MP and production of consumer goods is Division II of MP), the logical structure of the considered three blocks of the time budget is written down as follows.

AGGREGATE TIME OF THE POPULATION EMPLOYED IN MATERIAL PRODUCTION[*]

	Dialectical structure of the working time of the population employed in material production	Dialectical structure of the non-working time of the population employed in material production	Dialectical structure of the spare time of the population employed in material production
Thesis	Working time budget in the 1st MP subdivision	Non-working time budget in the 1st MP subdivision	Spare time budget of the population employed in the 1st MP subdivision
Antithesis	Working time budget in the 2nd MP subdivision	Non-working time budget in the 2nd MP subdivision	Spare time budget of the population employed in the 2nd MP subdivision
Synthesis	Aggregate working time budget of the 1st and 2nd MP subdivisions	Aggregate non-working time budget of the 1st and 2nd MP subdivisions	Aggregate spare time budget of the population employed on material production whole of 1st and 2nd subdivisions

[*]   In the first MP subdivision manufacturing the means of production takes place. Part of the means of production enters the second MP subdivision, part of it remains in the 1st MP subdivision, while part of it enters other spheres of production.

DIALECTICAL STRUCTURE OF THE AGGREGATE TIME OF POPULATION EMPLOYED IN INTELLECTUAL SPHERE

	Dialectical structure of the working time of the population employed in the intellectual sphere	Dialectical structure of the non-working time of the population employed in the intellectual sphere	Dialectical structure of the spare time budget of the population employed in the intellectual sphere
Thesis	Working time budget in the 1st division of the intellectual sphere	Non-working time budget in the 1st division of the intellectual sphere	Spare time budget of the population employed in the 1st division of the intellectual sphere
Antithesis	Working time budget in the 2nd and 3rd divisions of the intellectual sphere	Non-working time budget in the 2nd and 3rd divisions of the intellectual sphere	Spare time budget of the population employed in the 2nd and 3rd divisions of the intellectual sphere
Synthesis	Aggregate working time budget in the 1st, 2nd and 3rd divisions of the intellectual sphere	Aggregate non-working time budget in the 1st, 2nd and 3rd divisions of the intellectual sphere	Aggregate spare time budget of population employed on the whole of the 1st, 2nd and 3rd divisions of the intellectual sphere

DIALECTICAL STRUCTURE OF THE AGGREGATE TIME OF THE POPULATION EMPLOYED IN THE PUBLIC HEALTH SPHERE

	Dialectical structure of the working time of the population employed in the public health sphere	Dialectical structure of the non-working time of the population employed in the public health sphere	Dialectical structure of the spare time of the population employed in the public health sphere
Thesis	Working time budget in the 1st subdivision of the public health sphere	Non-working time budget in the 1st subdivision of the public health sphere	Spare time budget of the population employed in the 1st subdivision of the public health sphere
Antithesis	Working time budget in the 2nd subdivision of the public health sphere	Non-working time budget in the 2nd subdivision of the public health sphere	Spare time budget of the population employed in the 2nd subdivision of the public health sphere
Synthesis	Aggregate working time budget of the 1st and 2nd subdivisions of the public health sphere	Aggregate non-working time budget of the 1st and 2nd subdivisions of the public health sphere	Aggregate spare time budget of the population employed in the public health sphere in the 1st and 2nd subdivisions

DIALECTICAL STRUCTURE OF THE AGGREGATE TIME OF THE POPULATION EMPLOYED IN THE MILITARY SPHERE

	Dialectical structure of the working time of the population employed in the military sphere	Dialectical structure of the non-working time of the population employed in the military sphere	Dialectical structure of the spare time budget of the population employed in the military sphere
Thesis	Working time budget in the 1st subdivision of the military sphere	Non-working time budget in the 1st subdivision of the military sphere	Spare time budget of the population employed in the 1st subdivision of the military sphere
Antithesis	Working time budget in the 2nd subdivision of the military sphere	Non-working time budget in the 2nd subdivision of the military sphere	Spare time budget of the population employed in the 2nd subdivision of the military sphere
Synthesis	Aggregate working time budget of the 1st and 2nd subdivisions of the military sphere	Aggregate non-working time budget of the 1st and 2nd subdivisions of the military sphere	Aggregate spare time budget of the population employed in the military sphere in the 1st and 2nd subdivisions

DIALECTICAL STRUCTURE OF THE AGGREGATE TIME OF THE POPULATION EMPLOYED IN THE TRANSPORT SPHERE

	Dialectical structure of the working time of the population employed in the transport sphere	Dialectical structure of the non-working time of the population employed in the transport sphere	Dialectical structure of the spare time of the population employed in the transport sphere
Thesis	Working time budget in the 1st subdivision of the transport sphere	Non-working time budget in the 1st subdivision of the transport sphere	Spare time budget of the population employed in the 1st subdivision of the transport sphere
Antithesis	Working time budget in the 2nd subdivision of the transport sphere	Non-working time budget in the 2nd subdivision of the transport sphere	Spare time budget of the population employed in the 2nd subdivision of the transport sphere
Synthesis	Aggregate working time budget in the 1st and 2nd subdivisions of the transport sphere	Aggregate non-working time budget in the 1st and 2nd subdivisions of the transport sphere	Aggregate spare time budget of the population employed in the transport sphere in the 1st and 2nd subdivisions

LOGICAL STRUCTURE OF CALCULATING THE POTENTIAL BORDERS OF «ENLIGHTENMENT AND ENTERTAINMENT» MARKET

	Dialectical structure of the spare time of employees in the material sphere	Dialectical structure of the spare time of employees in the intellectual sphere	Dialectical structure of the spare time of employees in the public health sphere	Dialectical structure of the spare time of employees in the military sphere	Dialectical structure of the spare time of employees in the transport sphere	
Thesis	Spare time budget of the population employed in the 1st division of the material sphere	Spare time budget of the population employed in the 1st division of the intellectual sphere	Spare time budget of the population employed in the 1st division of the public health sphere	Spare time budget of the population employed in the 1st division of the military sphere	Spare time budget of the population employed in the 1st division of the transport sphere	Aggregate spare time budget of the population employed in the 1st division of the existing spheres of social production
Antithesis	Spare time budget of the population employed in the 2nd division of the material sphere	Spare time budget of the population employed in the 2nd and 3rd division of the intellectual sphere	Spare time budget of the population employed in the 2nd division of the public health sphere	Spare time budget of the population employed in the 2nd division of the military sphere	Spare time budget of the population employed in the 2nd division of the transport sphere	Aggregate spare time budget of the population employed in the 2nd division of the existing spheres of social production

Synthesis						
	Aggregate spare time budget of the population employed in the material sphere in the 1st and 2nd subdivisions	Aggregate spare time budget of the population employed in the intellectual sphere in the 1st, 2nd and 3rd divisions	Aggregate spare time budget of the population employed in the public health sphere in the 1st and 2nd divisions	Aggregate spare time budget of the population employed in the military sphere in the 1st and 2nd divisions	Aggregate spare time budget of the population employed in the transport sphere in the 1st and 2nd divisions	Aggregate spare time budget of the population employed in the 1st and 2nd divisions of the existing spheres of social production
	⇨	⇨	⇨	⇨	⇨	
	«Enlightenment and entertainment» market potential borders of those employed in the material sphere	«Enlightenment and entertainment» market potential borders of those employed in the intellectual production	«Enlightenment and entertainment» market potential borders of those employed in the public health sphere	«Enlightenment and entertainment» market potential borders of those employed in the military sphere	«Enlightenment and entertainment» market potential borders of those employed in the transport sphere	

«ENLIGHTENMENT AND ENTERTAINMENT» MARKET POTENTIAL LIMITS

CHAPTER 7

SEGMENT STRUCTURE OF THE «ENLIGHTENMENT AND ENTERTAINMENT» MARKET[31]

All political economists have long since concentrated on the questions of material production and removed the problems of the intellectual sphere from their investigations in political economics. Therefore «enlightenment and entertainment branches» developed in terms of unelaborated economic categories.

- first, what portion of the spare time of the people comes out as wealth of a society and what portion does not?
- second, what is the essence of the social and economic evaluation of the spare time of the people, that is considered wealth of a society?
- third, in what direction must the qualitative structure of the people's spare time be improved?

It is not possible to considerably improve effectiveness in planning, organizing and administrating the «enlightenment and entertainment branches» without getting correct and precise replies to the above. At the moment, spare time is not represented as a purposeful indicator in the branches under consideration. Their activities are indirectly reflected in the aggregate of the indices, used in the statistics. And in most cases it does not feature in decision making, either in organizing or in planning the activities of the branches or an individual institution.

---

31 The branch-wise indicator

I propose «time of the intellectual servicing of people» or duration of consuming the intellectual services to be used as a social index for the activities of the «enlightenment and entertainment branch» institutions. In my opinion, this unit of measurement is the only possible natural measure for the activity results of the «enlightenment and entertainment branch». The intellectual services cannot be measured in meters or kilograms, but by the time of their consumption. Their quantity depends on the number of individuals who are involved in a process of intellectual servicing. It also depends on the quality of the production technology, on the conditions of capital assets, labor resources and the willingness of visitors and listeners to consume the services.

The activities of the «enlightenment and entertainment branches» and institutions are intended to assimilate the resource of population's spare time. This must be met every day. An utilisation of the time indicator, while estimating the activities of the «enlightenment and entertainment branches», smoothes out the differing quality of these services. It also softens their specific character and leads to a unique measurement.

The other portion of people's spare time, which is left out of the socially arranged process, must not come out as «a measure for the wealth of society». Proceeding from the stated above, it is possible to write the following logical structure:

DIALECTICAL SCHEME OF PEOPLE'S SOCIALISING IN THEIR SPARE TIME IN THE «ENLIGHTENMENT AND ENTERTAINMENT BRANCHES»

Thesis   A socially productive labor in the «enlightenment and entertainment branches» is the labor that assimilates the population's spare time.

Antithesis A socially unproductive labor is the labor that does not enter a socially arranged production process of services in the «enlightenment and entertainment branches».

Synthesis   An aggregate labor in the «enlightenment and entertainment branches» is both a socially productive and a socially unproductive labor.

The above dialectical scheme reflects two inter-opposed processes: on the one hand, a socially arranged process and, on the other, a socially non-arranged process of creating intellectual services. An expansion of the borders of the first would lead to a reduction of the borders of the second and vice versa.

The activities of the «enlightenment and entertainment branches» are a specific type of socially arranged production process, directed to meet the people's immaterial-intellectual needs and those of society as a whole. Acceptance of the labor as productive is the basis for including the results of these activities in the aggregate results.

A. ASSIMILATION OF THE RESOURCE OF THE PEOPLE'S SPARE TIME BY THE MUSEUM BRANCH

I propose to estimate the social effects of art museums with the help of the time measurement. I conducted a survey of 2000 visitors. There was a question about how much time they spend in a museum. The computer sorted out the information obtained. The data is given below:

STRUCTURE OF THE VISITORS' FLOW INTO AN ART MUSEUM (AS PER DURATION OF VISIT)

Column of indicators	Duration of museum visit (minutes, hours)						
	15-20 min	21-30 min	31-40 Min	41-50 min	51-60 min	61-1hour 10 min	1hour 10 min -1hour 20min
Proportion of visitors, %	0.16	-	3.8	6	16.4	47.2	11.2

Column of indicators	Duration of museum visit (minutes, hours)						
	1h 31m- 1h 40m	1h 41 m- 1h 50 m	1h 51 m- 1h 60 m	2h 01m- 2h 10m	2h 11m- 2h 20m	2h 21m- 2h 30m	Over 2h 30m
Proportion of visitors, %	5	4.1	1	0.6	1	0.6	0.5

I propose the following calculation of the social effect for the activities of the
art museum staff according to the formula given below:

$$A_{STP} = \frac{\sum_{i=1}^{n} Ki \, (T_1 \cdot \Pi_C + T_2 \Pi_{\text{и}})}{}$$

in which

A_{STP}—the spare time resource of the visitors;

Ki—proportion of visitors as opposed to the I-duration of their visit;

T_1 and T_2—structure of local and foreign visitors in the context of the duration of their visit.

Π_C, $\Pi_{\text{и}}$—number of local and foreign visitors.

n— quantity of temporary gradations.

The calculation of the assimilated spare time resource of local visitors can be
done according to this table:

%			min	Thousands of people			
1.	0.16	X	20	X 178.4	=	95	hour
2.	3.80	X	36	X 178.4	=	3955	hour
3.	6.00	X	45	X 178.4	=	7028	hour
4.	15.40	X	55	X 178.4	=	25184	hour
5.	47.20	X	65	X 178.4	=	91222	hour
6.	11.20	X	75	X 178.4	=	24976	hour
7.	5.00	X	85	X 178.4	=	12637	hour
8.	4.10	X	95	X 178.4	=	11581	hour
9.	1.00	X	105	X 178.4	=	2122	hour
10.	0.60	X	115	X 178.4	=	2052	hour
11.	1.00	X	125	X 178.4	=	3717	hour
12.	0.60	X	135	X 178.4	=	2408	hour
13.	0.50	X	145	X 178.4	=	2156	hour
14.	0.50	X	155	X 178.4	=	2304	hour
15.	0.16	X	165	X 178.4	=	785	hour
					Total:	194 220	hour

The art museum staff assimilated 194,200 hours of the spare time (ST) of local visitors—38,800 hours in the city as a whole and 155,400 hours of the spare time of foreign visitors, i.e 20 per cent and 80 per cent respectively.

18,700 foreigners visited the art museum during the investigated year. The average duration of their stay in the museum was lees than one hour. Knowing the average number of foreign visitors and the duration of their visit to the museum, we can calculate the assimilated spare time resource of this group of visitors as 18,700 hours. If we add this to the assimilated spare time resource of local visitors, the art museum staff assimilate 213,000 hours of spare time, broken down into:

- guests—155,400 hours (73 per cent),
- citizens of the city—38,800 hours (18,2 per cent),
- foreign tourists—18,700 hours (8,8 per cent).

The proposed social estimation of the activity results for museums allows us to carry out precise calculations of the intellectual services produced in this branch.

ASSIMILATION OF THE RESOURCE OF THE PEOPLE'S SPARE TIME BY THE MUSEUM SYSTEM

Consumption of museum and exhibition services over 20 years

Index name	Years				
	1	5	10	15	19
Average consumption of museum and exhibition services per capita					
Weekly (min.)	0.64	0.60	0.80	1.00	1.00
annually (min.)	33.28	312.00	41.60	52.00	52.00
Population in millions	208.80	232.20	241.70	253.30	262.40
R million hours	115.80	120.70	167.60	219.50	227.40

B. ASSIMILATION OF THE RESOURCE OF THE PEOPLE'S SPARE TIME BY THE LIBRARY BRANCH

In my research of this group of institutions I proceed on the basis that an assimilated resource of the population's spare time is a guideline for their activities. Nikulin V.V. and Strunina O.N. express a similar thought: «*we chose the time spent on reading newspapers as a unit of measuring have consumed newspaper information. The time of consumption is individual and depends on education and personal habits. But these differences fade while investigating the aggregate information. Time can be used as an average indicator*». In my opinion, research of this assimilated resource is not enough. The assimilated resource of spare time is somehow taken out of the whole aggregate of economic categories. In reality it is just vice versa, i.e. this category must be linked to other categories.

This is the reason why we must consider the second portion of spare time, which is left out of the framework of the institutions of the intellectual sphere (including libraries). Proceeding from the above, we can write down the logical structure as follows:

DIALECTICAL SCHEME OF SOCIALISING THE PEOPLE'S ACTIVITIES IN THEIR SPARE TIME IN THE LIBRARY SPHERE

Thesis A portion of the people's spare time socialized by the staff of the libraries (book reading, reading periodicals of the library funds).

Antithesis A portion of the people's spare time non-socialized by the libraries (book reading and reading periodicals of the personal libraries).

Synthesis The aggregate portion of the people's spare time given to people to consume the informational services in and outside the framework of the socially arranged process of their production.

The above dialectical scheme reflects an organic connection of the two portions of spare time: an expansion of the borders for the socialized portion of people's spare time, naturally leads to a reduction in the borders of its second portion.

The proposed unit of measurement allowed me to carry out calculations at the Universal Science Library.

The first stage was to survey 1000 visitors. The questionnaire included a question about visitors' duration of stay in the library. The computer sorted out the information obtained. The data is given below:

STRUCTURE OF FLOW OF THE VISITORS TO THE UNIVERSAL SCIENCE LIBRARY (DURATION OF VISIT)

Column of indicators	Duration of library visit (minutes, hours)									
	less 30m	from 30m- to 1hour	1h- 1h30m	1h30m-1h45m	1h45m -2h15m	2h15m-2h30m	2h45m-3h	3h- 3h15m	3.15- 3.30	3.30- 3.45
Proportion of visitors, %	1.1	13.2	8.6	1.8	26.3	9.3	8	7.1	2.7	1.3

Column of indicators	Duration of library visit (minutes, hours)									
	3.45 -4.00	4.00 -4.15	4.15 -4.30	4.30 -5.00	5.00 -5.30	5.30 -6.00	6.00 -6.30	6.30 -7.00	7.00 -7.30	7.30 -8.00
Proportion of visitors, %	6.4	1.3	1.3	8.1	3.2	2.9	1.3	2.7	0.4	3

Knowing the structure of visitors in terms of the duration of their stay (see Table № 4.12) makes it easy to find out the amount of the spare time resource assimilated by the library's staff.

	%		Thousands of people.		Min.		Min.		Hours
1.	1.10	X	182	X	30	=	60060	=	1000
2.	13.20	X	182	X	45	=	1081080	=	18018
3.	8.60	X	182	X	90	=	1408680	=	23478
4.	1.80	X	182	X	105	=	343980	=	5733
5.	16.20	X	182	X	120	=	3559920	=	59332
6.	9.30	X	182	X	145	=	2453270	=	40904
7.	8.00	X	182	X	175	=	2548000	=	42467
8.	7.10	X	182	X	188	=	2429336	=	40490
9.	2.70	X	182	X	203	=	997542	=	16626
10.	1.30	X	182	X	217	=	1066338	=	16772
11.	6.40	X	182	X	233	=	2715984	=	45233
12.	1.30	X	182	X	248	=	586768	=	9880
13.	4.30	X	182	X	263	=	622259	=	10371
14.	8.10	X	182	X	285	=	4201470	=	70025
15.	3.20	X	182	X	315	=	1834560	=	30576
16.	2.00	X	182	X	345	=	1820912	=	30349
17.	1.30	X	182	X	375	=	887250	=	14786
18.	2.70	X	182	X	390	=	1916460	=	31941
19.	0.40	X	182	X	345	=	316680	=	5278
20.	0.40	X	182	X	465	=	2538900	=	42315
							Total:		**556 475**

Thus, according to my calculations, the library staff assimilated 556,475 hours (stationary) and another 200,000 hours of the people's spare time (with the help of subscription [approximate data]). The summary annual volume of the STP resource assimilated by the library's staff comes to 756,500 hours.

The given institution has developed a considerable bank of subscription of services offered to visitors, which considerably increases the social effect of staff activities.

C. ASSIMILATION OF THE PEOPLE'S SPARE TIME RESOURCE (STP) BY A COUNTRY'S LIBRARY SYSTEM

Having considered the problems of assimilating the spare time resource for the science library, I tried to calculate the values of these characteristics for the library system, as a whole.

The number of readers came to 116.2 million people and the number of books read comes to 1398.9 million.

If we proceed on the basis that the average time taken to read a book was 2.5 hours, the volume of the spare time resource assimilated by the libraries comes to:

1398.9 million copies x 2.5 hours = 3,500 million men-hours.

ASSIMILATION OF THE PEOPLE'S SPARE TIME RESOURCE (ASTP) BY «ENLIGHTENMENT AND ENTERTAINMENT» ENTERPRISES

ASSIMILATION OF THE SPARE TIME RESOURCE BY SPORTS-ENTERTAINMENT SERVICES

Index Name	Years				
Average per capita sports-entertainment services	1	5	10	15	19
weekly (min)	6	7	9	12	12
annually (min)	312	364	468	624	624
Population in millions	208.8	232.2	241.7	253.3	262.4
R (million hours)	1085.7	1408.7	1885.2	2634.3	2728.9

ASSIMILATION OF THE SPARE TIME RESOURCE BY CONCERT ENTERPRISES

Index Name	Years				
	1	5	10	15	19
Average consumption of concert enterprises per capita					
weekly min.	0.8	0.8	0.9	1.1	0.8
annually min.	48	48	49.4	66	48
Population in millions	208.8	232.2	241.7	253.3	262.4
R million hours	167	186	199	278	299

ASSIMILATION OF THE SPARE TIME RESOURCE BY THEATRES

Index Name	Years				
	1	5	10	15	19
Average consumption of theater services per capita					
weekly min.	1.3	1.4	1.4	1.4	1.41
annually min.	67.6	72.8	72.8	72.8	73.32
Population in millions	208.8	232.2	241.7	253.3	262.4
R million hours	235.2	281.7	293.2	307.3	320.6

At present there is an inaccuracy in calculating the number of visitors to the theatre and, as a result, in calculating the volumes of the assimilated STP resource. The inaccuracy comes in the fact that the theatre serves the «home» audience, while a touring theater group also plays in the city. This means that theatre can use its own premises to reach good social and economic activity results at the expense of high, professional skills of guest groups.

Estimation of the activities of the «enlightenment and entertainment branch», considered herewith, make it possible to organize, plan and administrate the production, distribution, exchange and consumption factors of this specific activity and its results, i.e. the intellectual services, in a principally new way.

D. ASSIMILATION OF THE SPARE TIME RESOURCE BY A CITY'S «ART» INSTITUTIONS

An analysis of the STP resource assimilated in a city by a network of art institutions reveals that theater and concert institutions assimilated 4.357 million hours of STP in the 1st year of investigation, broken down into:

	1st year	3rd year	7th year
The state philharmonic society	38.4%	37.2%	40.2%
Musical comedy	18.3%	16.1%	16.9%
Opera and ballet	17.1%	18.3%	16.3%
Theatre № 1	13.0%	13.5%	9.8%;
Theatre № 2	8.2%	8.9%	9.4%
The young people's theatre	5.0%	6.0%	7.4%
Total	100%	100%	100%

The structure of the given theatre services changed within seven years as follows.

ASSIMILATION OF THE STP RESOURCE BY THEATER INSTITUTIONS OF A CITY DURING A 7 YEAR PERIOD (in hours)

Index Name	Years							
	0	1	2	3	4	5	6	6/0
1. Theater № 1 including:	357.70	388.50	386.20	405.90	360.70	398.50	407.50	113.9%
stationary	273.10	294.20	311.50	261.60	201.40	256.70	222.00	81.3%
on tour	84.60	97.20	74.20	144.30	159.30	141.70	185.50	219.2%
2. Theater № 2 including:	568.00	585.00	586.00	487.00	381.00	432.00	424.00	74.7%
stationary	339.00	346.00	365.00	294.00	265.00	340.00	297.00	87.6%
on tour	229.00	239.00	221.00	193.00	16.00	192.00	127.00	55.4%
3. Opera	744.00	753.00	793.00	759.00	686.00	703.00	707.00	95.0%

including:								
stationary	737.00	741.00	790.00	751.50	680.00	695.50	691.50	94.0%
on tour	7.00	12.00	3.00	7.50	6.00	7.50	16.50	220.0%
4. Musical Comedy	797.00	897.00	700.00	710.00	730.00	726.00	735.00	81.9%
including:								
stationary	459.00	459.00	661.00	673.00	637.00	571.00	594.00	129.0%
on tour	438.00	438.00	39.00	44.00	93.00	155.00	141.00	32.0%
5. State Philharmonic society	1674	1539	1612	1825	1878	1668	1740	103.90%
including:								
stationary	765	607	510	642	710	618	620	81.0%
on tour	909	932	1102	1183	1168	1050	1120	123.3%
6. Young Spectators Theater	216	208	263	297	280	241	322	149%
including:								
stationary	180	189	199	202	214	175	—	—
on tour	36	19	64	95	66	66	322	8 times
Total:	**4357**	**4371**	**4652**	**4491**	**4316**	**4168**	**4335**	**99.5%**

Theatre № 1 increases the borders of assimilating the STP resource from 357,700 hours to 407,500 hours, i.e. by 13.9 per cent every year. Moreover, the permanent volume of services decreased by 18.7 per cent and increased 2,2 times while on tour.

The assimilation of the STP resource by Theatre № 2 fell by 25.3 per cent within six years—on permanent staging by 12.4 per cent and on tour by 44.6 per cent.

If the volume of theatre services given to people in the Ukrainian language is measured with the entire volume, one can see that their proportion decreased from 13 per cent down to 9.8 per cent in the period under consideration.

OPERA AND BALLET

The theatre assimilated 744,000 men-hours of STP in the basic year, including 737,000 hours and—7,000 hours while on tour.

On the whole, theater activities decreased by 5 per cent over the period in question. M.Naydorf explained the main reasons for this decline. His article «What to listen to at the Opera?» notes the declining quality of productions given that «the first staging is not made for its visitor—a viewer» but for a special date, for extra money or just to satisfy regional bosses. For instance, the theatre showed «Mozart and Solierie», an Opera by Rymsky Korsakov, 40 times in one year. Ten spectacles were staged three times a year. I do not know whether it is possible to count the plays shown every three or four months in the theatres. I do not think it is possible to keep a play's «living soul» when it is performed at such intervals.

MUSICAL COMEDY

The volume of the assimilated STP resource by musical comedy came to 900,000 hours, including 51 per cent on permanent stage and 49 per cent on tour in the first year. Such a high «on tow» proportion of assimilation is explained by the fact that the theatre was then under repair and its administration maximized the touring opportunities.

The theatre staff worked in its new building in the third year. That year the volume of the assimilated resource of people's spare time (while on tour) decreased by 400,000 hours. At the same time the resource assimilation from permanent staging increased by 223,000 hours. Such an increase was mainly due to the fact that the number of seats in the theatre rose from 570 to 1,319 and was made considerably more comfortable.

The volume of the services given by the theatre as whole was 82 per cent of the first year.

STATE PHILHARMONIC ORCHESTRA

The highest assimilation of the STP resource by the State Philharmonic Orchestra was 1,878 hours in the fifth year of the period under consideration. The level increased by 3.9 per cent over a six year period including an 123.2 per cent increase by while on tour. The values of permanent fixtures decreased by 19 per cent.

This can be explained by the fact that the price of a one man-hour ticket for permanent fixtures did not change for six years. The price of tickets while on tour went up by 28 per cent over three years.

THE YOUNG PEOPLE'S THEATRE

The Young People's Theatre (YPT) increased its volume of theatre services by 1.5 times over the seven years. A proportion of the permanent and touring services came to 75.7 per cent to 24.3 per cent respectively in the first year. The following year the theatre was closed for repair. Its staff completely altered the activities and they started to go on tour. An assimilation of the STP resource increased eight fold under these conditions.

ASSIMILATION OF THE SPARE TIME RESOURCE BY A COUNTRY'S THEATRES

Index Name	Years				
	1	5	10	15	19
Average per capita consumption of cinema services comes to:					
weekly (minutes)	38.9	42.8	44.2	40.8	36.5
annually (minutes)	2022.8	2225.6	2298.4	2121.6	1898
(hours)	33.71	37.09	38.3	35.36	31.6
Size of population					
(millions)	208,8	232,2	241.7	253.3	262.4
	(1959)	(1966)			
including: urban	100	123.7	136	151.9	1636.6
country	108.8	108.5	105.7	101.4	166.2
R (million hours)	7038.6	8612.3	9257.1	8956.7	8291.8

ASSIMILATION OF THE SPARE TIME OF THE POPULATION IN A CITY BY THE CINEMA (in thousand hours)

Name of cinema halls	YEARS						
	1	2	3	4	5	6	7
Cinema № 1	3732	3504	3614	2844	2839	2750	3107
Cinema № 2	2782	117	1425	2453	2414	2443	2136
Cinema № 3	2326	2708	2387	2145	1894	1885	1813
Cinema № 4	2184	2196	2382	2218	2033	2091	2009
Cinema № 5	1560	1778	1711	1598	1604	1766	1837

Cinema № 6	1732	1785	1497	1460	1341	1309	826
Cinema № 7	1582	1657	1890	1828	1630	1463	1156
Cinema № 8	940	1273	1218	852	640	656	558
Cinema № 9	1287	1258	950	444	1035	952	873
Cinema № 10	1140	1181	1102	874	759	701	575
Cinema № 11	1140	1161	1094	1118	1127	994	870
Cinema № 12	1011	1189	1148	958	901	890	847
Cinema № 13	700	901	682	635	602	523	429
Cinema № 14	894	853	824	692	585	538	398
Cinema № 15	780	848	767	749	727	745	640
Cinema № 16	814	772	753	726	647	620	379
Cinema № 17	657	642	632	559	577	608	598
Cinema № 18	715	705	717	758	804	764	715
Cinema № 19	383	402	360	386	372	365	287
Cinema № 20	301	281	70	63	346	356	237
Cinema № 21	320	351	325	300	275	259	194
Cinema № 22	424	443	414	407	418	371	336
Cinema № 23	32	25	21	—	—	—	—
TOTAL:	27450	26037	25932	24015	23573	23055	20824
%	100%	94.8%	94.4%	87.5%	85.5%	84.0%	75.8%

«TV BROADCASTING» AND «RADIO BROADCASTING»

The products of labor of the «TV Broadcasting» and «Radio Broadcasting» branches are different from other products of labor as they produce an immaterial form of service. **This is the first peculiar feature.**

The second peculiar feature of the labor product of «TV Broadcasting» and «Radio Broadcasting» is that the production and consumption of the services coincide in time. This fact allows us to **use «time» as a unit of measurement** that must calculate the social result of these branches' activities.

Time spent viewing or listening, as a unit of measurement, in the volumes of the service production by «TV Broadcasting» and «Radio Broadcasting» made it possible for me to carry out the calculations given below.

DISTRIBUTION OF SPECTATORS DEPENDING ON LENGTH OF REVIEW

Index Name	Length of time spent watching TV programs per week-day (in minutes)							
	0	1-59	60-119	120-179	180-239	240-299	300-359	>360
Men	58.8	12.3	12.2	13.5	2.5	0.7	0.0	0.0
Women	69.5	10.6	12.0	16.8	0.8	0.3	0.0	0.0
Average length time spent watching TV (minutes)	0.0	30.0	89.5	149.5	209.5	269.5	329.5	>329.5

We can calculate the assimilated STP resource by «Television» for the male and female population on weekdays,[32] based on table № 4.19, in the following way:

MEN:

									average length
in millions	%	in millions		in millions		in minutes			in hours
54.1	x	12.3	x	30.0	=	199.5		=	3.32
54.1	x	12.2	x	89.5	=	590.7		=	9.84
54.1	x	13.5	x	149.5	=	2022.7		=	33.70
54.1	x	2.5	x	209.5	=	283.3		=	4.72
54.1	x	0.7	x	269.5	=	102.0		=	1.70
								Total	**53.28**

---

32 V. Patrushev «Aggregated time of society», p.188

WOMEN: average
                                                              length
                        in mil-
in millions % lions   in million   in minutes   in hours
52.76   X 10.6   x   30.0 =   167.7   =   2.80
52.76   X 12.0   x   89.5 =   566.5   =   9.40
52.76   X 6.8   x 149.5 =   535.2   =   8.90
52.76   X 0.8   x 209.5 =   88.0   =   1.46
52.76   X 0.3   x 269.5 =   43.1   =   0.72
                                                       Total   **23.28**

If we proceed on the basis that there is a 5-day working week 240 working days
in a year, then we can calculate the volume of consumed TV services on
weekdays, by the urban population, as follows:

Men (week-days)   *53.28 million hours x 240 days = 12.8 billion hours*
Women (week-days)   *23.28 million hours x 240 days = 5.58 billion hours*

The volume of consumption of audio and visual TV services at weekends could
be as follows:

DISTRIBUTION OF TV WATCHERS DEPENDING ON LENGTH OF REVIEW

Index Name	Length of telecast review (minutes) at weekends							
	0	1-59	60-119	120-179	180-239	240-299	300-359	>360
Weekends								
men								
on Saturdays	53.2	6.9	16.3	10.8	9.9	2.9	0.0	-
on Sundays	48.0	4.9	16.3	13.8	9.9	4.0	4.0	-
women								
on Saturdays	58.6	6.9	23.1	5.7	5.2	0.5	0.0	—
on Sundays	59.3	6.1	18.0	10.3	4.0	2.3	0.0	—
Average length of review of telecast								
(minutes)	0.0	30.0	89.5	149.5	209.5	269.5	329.5	—

Using table № 4.22, we can calculate the volume of the assimilated spare time resource of the working urban population at weekends:

Men (Saturdays)

in millions %	in millions	in million	in minutes	average length in hours
54.1	x 6.9	x 30.0	= 111.9 =	1.87
54.1	x 16.3	x 89.5	= 789.2 =	13.15
54.1	x 10.8	x 149.5	= 873.5 =	14.56
54.1	x 9.9	x 209.5	= 1122.0 =	18.70
54.1	x 2.9	x 269.5	= 423.1 =	7.00
			Total:	**55.18**

Men (Sundays)

in millions %	in millions	in million	in minutes	average length in hours
54.1 x	4.6	x 30.0	= 74.7 =	1.25
54.1 x	16.3	x 89.5	= 787.6 =	13.12
54.1 x	13.8	x 149.5	= 1115.3 =	18.60
54.1 x	9.9	x 209.5	= 1120.8 =	18.70
54.1 x	4.0	x 269.5	= 582.1 =	9.70
54.1 x	4.0	x 329.5	= 711.7 =	11.80
			Total:	**73.17**

If we proceed on the basis that there are 240 working days a year, with 5-day working weeks, and that there are 52 weekends, plus 21 public holidays, then the volume of TV consumption comes to:

on Saturdays
> *52.2 million hours x 52 Saturdays = 2,807.4 million hours*

on Sundays
> *73.1 million hours x 52 Sundays = 3,801.2 million hours*

On the assumption that the time budget for public holidays is similar to the time budget structure on Saturdays, we can calculate the volume of TV consumption on these days as:

$$52.2 \ x \ 21 = 1,159.2 \ million \ hours$$

The total volume of the assimilated spare time resource of the urban male population on weekends and holidays is as following:

2.81 billion hours + 3.80 billion hours +1.16 billion hours = 7.77 billion hours

The total volume of the assimilated STP resource for the urban female population on weekends and holidays is calculated as follows:

Women (Saturdays)

in millions %		in millions	in million	average length in minutes		in hours
52.76	x 6.9	x 30.0	= 109.2	=	1.82
52.76	x 23.1	x 89.5	= 1090.1	=	18.16
52.76	x 5.7	x 149.5	= 448.5	=	7.47
52.76	x 5.2	x 209.5	= 574.0	=	9.56
52.76	x 0.5	x 269.5	= 70.0	=	1.16
				Total:	**38.17**

Women (Sunday)

in millions %		in millions	in million	average length in minutes		in hours
52.76	x 6.1	x 30.0	= 96.5	=	1.61
52.76	x 18.0	x 89.5	= 849.9	=	14.16
52.76	x 10.3	x 149.5	= 812.4	=	13.54
52.76	x 4.0	x 209.5	= 442.1	=	7.37
52.76	x 2.3	x 269.5	= 545.0	=	9.08
				Total:	44.15

TV consumption by workingwomen, in one year, came to:

on Saturdays: *38,17 million hours x 52 days = 1.98 billion hours*
on Sundays: *44,15 million hours x 52 days = 2.29 billion hours*
on holidays: *38,17 million hours x 21 days = 0.80 billion hours*

The total volume of the assimilated STP resource of women by TV is calculated in the following manner:

1.98 billion hours + 2.29 billion hours + 0.80 billion hours =
= 5.08 billion hours

The total volume of the assimilated STP resource by «Television» on weekdays and at weekends:

men—*12.8 billion hours x 7.76 billion hors = 20.56 billion hours*
women—*5.58 billion hours + 5.08 billion hours = 10.64 billion hours*
Total: 31.2 billion hours

The spare time resource of the urban population commanding by «Broadcasting» is:

men *20.56 billion hours x 3% = 616.8 million hours*
women   *10.64 billion hours x 3% = 319.2 million hours*
Total: 936 million hours

E. CALCULATION OF THE SPARE TIME RESOURCE OF THE RURAL POPULATION ASSIMILATED BY «TELEVISION»

Time spent by the population in watching telecasts and listening to broadcasts per annum to:
men—352.5 hours
women—273 hours

Knowing the number of inhabitants in the country (97.9 million), we can calculate the relevant volumes of assimilated STP resource as:

men - *39 million people x 352.5 hours = 13.75 billion hours*
women - *41 million people x 273 hours = 11.2 billion hours*

The total volume of the STP resource assimilated by «Television» and «Broadcasting» in rural areas comes to:
24.2 billion hours x 97 % of the population involved

Radio broadcast services came to 3% of this value:

24.2 billion hours x 3% = 726 million hours

The volume of television services watched by countryside is:

24.2 billion hours—276 million hours = 23.47 billion hours

The calculations of the STP resource assimilated by the «enlightenment and entertainment branches», which this book has tried to be set out, makes it possible to construct a general structure of the «enlightenment and entertainment» market.

SEGMENT STRUCTURE OF THE COUNTRY'S «ENLIGHTENMENT AND ENTERTAINMENT» MARKET

BRANCH	Assimilated resource STP	Percentage Ratio
Museums	227.4 million hours	0.32%
Concert Enterprises	299 million hours	0.42%
Theaters	320.6 million hours	0.45%
Libraries	3500 million hours	5.00%
Cinemas	8291 million hours	11.80%
Broadcasting	1834 million hours	2.60%
Television	55400 million hours	79.31%
TOTAL:	**69873 million hours**	100%

CHAPTER 8

ECONOMIC PROBLEMS IN THE «ENLIGHTENMENT AND ENTERTAINMENT BRANCHES»

A. THE NEGATIVE PECULIARITIES OF ORGANIZATION OF THE ENLIGHTENMENT AND ENTERTAINMENT BRANCHES

If we consider the «enlightenment and entertainment branches» as a socio-economic system, we should first establish what the aims of its branches are functioning the principles of the interaction of all its elements horizontally, as well as vertically and the principles of its internal organization and functions.

Out of this arises the question of the direction in which society organizes its «entertainment branch»:

—Whether or not the aim of enterprises in this sphere is to extract as big a profit as possible;

—Or whether this sphere aims to attract as many visitors as possible at a minimum price of entry?

It would be wrong to give an affirmative answer to any of these questions. So to avoid distorting approaches towards answering them, we will analyze the aim indicators of the «enlightenment and entertainment branches».

At the moment the obvious aims of the activities practiced by branches of «Culture», «Art», «Religious» institutions, «Sports-entertainment», «Television» and «Broadcasting» are «attendance», «TV-watchers» and «radio-listeners». These indicators reflect people's presence in the process of intellectual servicing. But their application leads to certain statistical errors in result sheets. In the «enlightenment and entertainment branches», as in other branches, the optimal state must be shared for and realized by minimizing in-put costs. For a long time this principle was not realized because «the result» function was substituted for «the expenditure» function, which creates a paradox. The worse a «enlightenment and entertainment» institution works, naturally, the larger the cost of production, and, respectively, the higher the number of services rendered to the intellectual well being of the people. In other words, the worse these institutions work, the better it is for us. Unequivocal reflection of the aims of these development within of these branches the entire national economy means that in practice, organs that organize, plan and manage these branches are only formally responsible for economic processes occurring within them, sure to entail negative economic and social consequences.

The above shortcomings in determining the aims of the «enlightenment and entertainment branches» have caused a considerably disproportional development of fixed assets and labor resources and distribution of these activities among the various regional demographic groups of the population in our country.

While considering the principle of commensurability of results with expenditure one must also draw attention to another feature. The level of «enlightenment and entertainment branches» is estimated according to the following criteria:

$$K_1 = \frac{n}{MC}; \quad K_2 = \frac{S}{MC}; \quad K_3 = \frac{S - R_{real}}{MC}.$$

in which
  n—number of visitors
  S—subsidies from the state budget
  MC—material costs
  R_{real}—financial receipts

If we carry out an analysis of the activities of «enlightenment and entertainment branches» on the basis of the above criteria, then their criteria values may be increased or reduced. However, complexity comes in the following. If we analyze the level of organization of «Culture» institutions on the basis of the first criterion, «Art», on the basis of the second and «Television», on the basis of the third, the problem lies in conjugating the criteria (the first, second, and third) among themselves. In such case, there may arise the situation in which one group of «enlightenment and entertainment branches» achieved great results, calculated by the first criterion, and a second group of institutions, by the second criterion. The question naturally arises, which one of them is better? Here, scientific researchers should express opinions. Unfortunately, they refuse to take any part in working out theoretical principles of organization of the «enlightenment and entertainment branches».

The joint study on the problems of «Culture» by two economic masters, T.L. Klyachko and T. V. Shokhina, proposed a very interesting indicator of the efficiency of category services, in its eighth chapter:[33]

$$l = \frac{O_1 - O_2}{O_3}$$

in which

O_1—payable services in the gross proceeds

O_2—free services

O_3—conditional net production of the service sphere.

The shortcomings of this indicator are as follows:

The first—the numerator is **a sum of the cost of payable services,** which, as it is known, is measured in dollars, and **the amount of free services**, which until recently has been measured in attendance. These two values O_1 and O_2 cannot be combined because they are heterogeneous. This arithmetic problem can only be solved if the added values are homogenous.

The second—there are other illogical mistakes. For example, they suggest that the absurd numerator should be divided by the even more absurd

---

33 T.L.Klyachko. T.V. Shokhina. Their monograph «Culture and means of the mass information (social and economic problems)». Economics, p. 99.

«conditional indicator» (O_3) is labeled the «conditional net production of the service sphere» is this what you mean here?

While proposing to use an indicator of «clear production of service sphere», these economists have not established the following factors:
—Amount of services rendered by this sphere;
—No structure of a category's services has been determined for public health, the ministry of internal affairs, the army, etc.
—Components of a service have not determined past labor and surplus products in the service sphere.

Without knowledge of these factors it would be incorrect to introduce conditional clear production into the organization, planning and management of the service sphere.

If an intermediate conclusion, we can point out that a restriction on solving the problem is the very low degree of reflection of «enlightenment and entertainment branches» processes in the existing aggregate of indicators. Thus, they do not play the role they are given in the organization of institutional activities.[34]

An absence of economic theory leads to high practical expenses. For example, film distribution enterprises pay the following taxes in some countries: taxes on capital and circulating assets: 2-5 per cent; income tax: 7-13 per cent; social insurance tax: 7 per cent; profit tax: 55 per cent. In other words, the total tax payable by film distributors comes to nearly 80 per cent of the money made from selling cinema art. **Such a tax policy is overwhelming;** it does not assist an optimal development of enterprise. In most cases, the taxes are not graduated according to the number of visitors, the number of employees or the amount of profit. How can a system develop if 70-80 per cent of its receipts are paid on taxes?

Utilization of such system of administrating the «enlightenment and entertainment branches» for many decades has been impossible for two reasons. Firstly there is no elementary economic conception of the mechanism in which the entertainment branches functions, and secondly the murderous taxation policy applied to this sphere is totally destructive.

---

34 However, one should note, that not all entertainment institutions are profitable, after all a considerable part of revenue (apart from heavy taxation) is «blown» on management and administration staff; the cost of staging performances is too large and actors are only partially employed during the year, etc.

Some of the investigations of the economic systems use the «entropy», which to a certain extent reflects the vitality (or destruction) of the inner structures of a system. An investigation of the entropy of the economic systems of the «entertainment branches» would expand our knowledge on the state of its chains, interaction, etc. We believe that this is one of the necessary directions to take in order to understand the processes taking place in the «entertainment branches».

B. MODERN STATE OF THE «ENLIGHTENMENT AND ENTERTAINMENT BRANCHES» DISTRIBUTION MECHANISM

I will now analyze the distribution mechanism of museum institutions, a powerful economic system. Over the last 20-25 years, the number of museums increased from 954 to 2,132 in the country under investigation. The museums' fixed asset value is estimated at tens of billions of US dollars, their maintenance expenditure is huge. Several tens of thousands of workers staff the museums while the number of visitors exceeded 198 million. In other words, this is a large economic system. The branch uses huge material and intellectual resources.

Many theoretical features of the development of this branch still have not been worked out today, namely:

-The aggregate of indicators of planning museum activities has not changed since the 1920s;

-The mechanism of distribution of museum institutions throughout the country is inadequate;

-Results of museum activities are not estimated from both social and economic points of view;

-Special features of the economic relations within the museum business have not been worked out, etc.

-Rational economic principles of material and intellectual values are absent.

As confirmation of the above, we can analyze the distribution production factors in the museum branch. The basis of the distribution mechanism of museum institution activities is an aggregate of indicators (criteria), which are used in selecting a variant of their development. For instance, general indicators of the state of the museum network appear as:

$$\text{Indicator №} 1 = \frac{\text{Area of the country (republic) in km}^2}{\text{Number of museums in the country (republic)}}$$

$$\text{Indicator №} 2 = \frac{\text{Size of country's population (republic)}}{\text{Number of museums in the country}}$$

If indicator № 1 is used to develop a network of museum institutions, then they should be built in either Kazakhstan or Turkmenistan, since these republics are the last places as regards provision of museums per thousand square kilometers.

If indicator № 1 calculates territories and regions, the museums must be built first of all on the peninsula of Jamal, or on the Siberian plane, where population density is one of two people per thousand square miles. The shortcomings of such an indicator are obvious—why should one build museums where people do not live?

If indicator № 2 is an absolute orienting point for museum development, then they should be built first in Uzbekistan or Turkmenistan, because the population density per museum, in these republics, is minimal. The disadvantage of this indicator is that it does not distinguish between large museums and second and third class museums.

I have shown two possible versions of developing the museum network. However, that is not all. There may be more if other indicators and criteria are used. Thus, a third indicator could be as follows:

$$\text{Indicator №} 3 = \frac{\text{Number of visitors to a republic}}{\text{Size of a republic's population}}$$

This indicator does not account for attendance time in a museum, which may vary from 15 minutes to four hours; it only reflects the fact of a person's involvement in the process of the service, no more than that.

$$\text{Indicator №} 4 = \frac{\text{Total attendance}}{\text{Aggregate expenses of a museum}}$$

$$\text{Indicator No 5} = \frac{\text{Number of attendees}}{\text{Number of staff}}$$

$$\text{Indicator No 6} = \frac{\text{Number of attendees over a year}}{\text{A museum's productive area in m}^2}$$

$$\text{Indicator No 7} = \frac{\text{Number of attendees over a year}}{\text{Balanced cost of an institution in dollars}}$$

Because of low quality «attendance» they also reflect a weak level of organization in the museum business. However, they are closer to the economic criteria as regards inner structure of building.

Another group is also close to the economic criteria:

$$\text{Indicator No 8} = \frac{\text{Indication No 1 (size of republic)}}{\text{Average maintenance expenses of one conditionally calculated museum}}$$

$$\text{Indicator No 9} = \frac{\text{Indication No 1 (size of republic)}}{\text{Number of museum employees (total salary in dollars)}}$$

$$\text{Indicator No 10} = \frac{\text{Indication No 1 (size of republic)}}{\text{Balanced cost of fixed assets of a museum in dollars}}$$

If we take the indicators No 1-10 as a basis for long-term planning, development and placement of museums, then there will be a considerable number of «optimal» versions.

PROVISION OF MUSEUMS BY REPUBLIC

Republic	Number of museums per 1000 km	Rank of provision	Number of museums per 1000 people	Rank of provision
Russia	13	9	145	9
Ukraine	3.2	7	265	12
Belorussia	2.3	6	109	7
Uzbekistan	10	8	377	15
Kazakhstan	48	12	263	11
Georgia	0.7	2	47	4
Azerbaijan	1.6	5	114	8
Litva	0.8	3	44	3
Latvia	1	4	40	2
Kirgizstan	18	10	336	13
Tajikistan	13	9	363	14
Moldova	0.6	1	70	6
Armenia	0.6	1	63	5
Turkmenistan	35	11	214	10
Estonia	0.8	3	26	1

The above «semi-economic» criteria establish some socio-economic processes, which occur in the development of museums, to a certain extent. However, we cannot be satisfied with this semi-knowledge. It is obvious that management of museums must be built on the basis of indicators and criteria, which reflect adequately the inner stage of their organization and should be well grounded from a political and economic point of view.

C. TERRITORIAL DISTRIBUTION OF FIXED ASSETS AND LABOR RESOURCES IN «CULTURE»

The following indicators are a basis for the distribution mechanism for club institutions:

1.   Number of all club institutions in all cities and regions.

2.   Distribution of club institutions in cities and regions, by type.
3.   Characteristics of the state of club institution buildings in cities and regions:
     a. Renovated,
     b. In need of repair,
     c. In disarray.
4.   Number of club institutions with auditoriums.
5.   Number of seats in all the auditoriums.
6.   Number of club institutions with main auditoriums:
     a. Up to 100 seats,
     b. From 100 to 300 seats,
     c. Over 300 seats.
7.   Number of musical instruments and the technical means possessed by club institutions (in cities and regions).
8.   Number of seats in all auditoriums of club institutions calculated per 1000 inhabitants.

In order to establish the weak and strong points of these indicators, we will analyze the placement (distribution) of the fixed assets of club institutions in Moldova, as a basis.

The minimum number of club institutions in the region was as follows: Chadyr-Lung—12, (3.5 times fewer than in: Ungeny—75, Orgeev—68, Faleshty—73). The uneven placement of this kind of cultural institution may be specified by applying the indicators of renovation (3).

The highest level of renovated club institutions was in the following regions: Kotovsk—56.6 per cent, Nisporeny—52.8 per cent, Kamensk—50.7 per cent, Kantemir—49.4 per cent. The figures show that despite the lowest number of club institutions being in Chadyr-Lung, only one is not renovated and that the rest have good material and technical provisions.

An analysis of the territorial distribution of club institutions, on the basis of their accommodation, reveals the weak points of the cultural and educational distribution mechanism. Thus, the average maximum seating of one club institution is as follows in the following regions:

a)   Slobodzeya—390 seats;
b)   Vulkaneshty—380 seats;
c)   Chadyr-Lung—327 seats;
d)   Komrat—311 seats;
e)   Brichany—310 seats;
f)   Grigoriopol—300 seats.

Indicators of auditorium seating, together with the number of people inhabiting their localities reveals the weak points mentioned earlier for organization of this branch. For instance, in the Chadyr-Lung region, average seating in one club institution amounted to 327 seats, a rather high indicator. However, if it is re-calculated per 1000 people, the number is reduced to 90, the lowest level in the republic.

The shortcomings in club institutions' development and distribution are intensified by migration. The value of the indicator rejecting seats per 1000 people increases in areas where the population builds up and decreases in the emptying localities. The values of these indicators decrease in the extending localities.

While working out building and construction plans in a region, architects do not keep to republic norms, but are guided by the principles of developing a network of club and other institutions in the intellectual sphere. Therefore, I determined the value of over expenditure on club institution building, up on the basis of the «List of standard designs on civil building in Moldova S.P—7, MSSR, S.P 264-12-89, 265-12-55, 265-12-112». (See Table № 3.2)

PROJECT ACCOMMODATION EXCEEDING THE NORM

Region, village	Calculated need of the population (in seats)	Building (calculated in seats)	Size of excess (on seats)	Value of over-expenditure. (in thousand dollars)
Dondushan region village Braikovo	80	300	220	153
village New Tatarovka	80	200	120	90
Kantemir region village Enikoy	220	600	380	637
Kamensky region village Grushka	220	600	380	637
Kriulyany region village Jevreny	210	400	190	100
Grigoriopol region village Gyrtop	240	600	360	600
Floreshty region village Nikolaevka	210	600	390	50

Soroksky region				
village Voronkovo	240	600	360	600
village Dubno	170	600	430	720
village Derkautsy	240	600	360	600
Sum-total:				**4.787**

Building club institutions with increased accommodation in small localities increases disproportional development of productive forces of this kind. Such an irrational building of clubs leads to an excessive provision of seats and over expenditure in the «Culture» branch, which could be distributed and used more rationally elsewhere.

In addition, building of club institutions with less seats than the norm also takes place (Table № 3.3).

UNDER-FINANCING OF CAPITAL ASSETS IN THE DEVELOPMENT OF THE «CULTURE» BRANCH

Region, village	Seats build	Seats needed
Kagulski region village Tatareshty	600	740
Nisporeny region village Boldureshty	400	700
Novoanensky region village Pugacheny	600	780
Resinsky region village alchedar	200	430
Ryshkensky region village Recha	400	650

Two average statistical criteria—a basis for the analysis of club provision in Moldova are given below, as regards specialists of higher and specialized cultural education (Table № 3.4).

INDICATORS OF DISTRIBUTION OF MOLDOVA «CULTURE» EXPERTS

Indicator heading	As per specialist of cultural education		Number of specialists per club institution
	higher	specialized	
City	15,960	8,200	5,07
Village	40,500	4,000	0,7
Republic	35,650	3,800	1,27

An analysis of the data in the tables enlightenment and shows a considerable difference between the average provision of specialists in higher and specialized cultural education: in the first case—2.5 times fewer (40,500/15,960), in the second case—twice as many (8,200/4,000).

The difference in provision of creative workers in clubs was 13.7 times (5.5 specialists per club in the city of Rybnitsa and 0.4 in the city of Kagul). In the nine largest cities of the republic, maximum provision was in the Strashenski region (0.62 specialist per club institution) and the minimum in Ungenski and Faleshtski regions (0.01 specialists per club). The difference between these two levels is 62 times!

A comparison of the maximum provision of specialists in Rybnitsa (5.5) with the minimum value of the same criterion in Ungenski and Faleshtski (0.01) shows a highly uneven distribution of workers with special cultural education in Moldova (5.5/0.01-550).

This given analysis of distribution of the material resources and labor forces in the «Culture» branch reflects the negative special features of distribution relations, which have formed in it.

But the results of our analysis may be made more accurate with the help of other statistical methods. However, in this case, the shortcomings cannot be overcome. In conclusion, one should note that the level of uneven distribution of capital assets and employees in «Culture» is a complicated sum that becomes more complex and significant, as the factors of production interact as a system. As a result, defects in the development of each of them multiply and the disproportion occurs. In other words, the total uneven development is far higher than the simple sum of disproportion as per factor of production taking part in the creation of intellectual services.

The situation demands that the distribution mechanism of this branch of the national economy be improved, urgently.

D. ANALYSIS OF THE EFFECTIVE CRITERIA IN THE «ENLIGHTENMENT AND ENTERTAIN-MENT BRANCHES»

We researched the qualitative criteria of efficiency of intellectual activities as follows:
—working out a criteria of efficiency for intellectual activities;
—working out a quantitative criteria for intellectual activities;
—building up socio-economic efficiency criteria;

P. V. Posdnyakov divided the first approach into two types as follows:
a) criteria of knowledge efficiency, cognition activity, consciousness orientation;
b) criteria reflecting practical activities of the population, namely labor, social activities.

Mr. A. I. Yakovlev supports a similar classification noting in his book that there are no special works at the moment, which would reveal the efficiency of intellectual ideological work as a whole: «a question of efficiency criteria remains debatable». In his opinion, «as efficiency of intellectual work should take a degree of scientific cognition of objective reality, formation of consciousness, social activity of people». However, the author gave no recommendation for the realization of these tasks. Please note that in his monograph, together with his statement about the necessity of working out efficiency criteria, A. I. Yakovlev expresses a negative attitude towards formalizing intellectual process and applying mathematical methods: «mathematical attempt of solving this problem is premature...». I cannot agree with such a point of view because the quality of any activity improves if thoroughly calculated, or if a plan of operations is worked out, etc. Besides, using precise methods reveals both weak and strong points in the organization of any process, including immaterial-intellectual ones.

Other researchers of qualitative estimation of efficiency of immaterial intellectual activities propose to determine it by a degree of realization of set tasks. Comparison of aim with what is actually achieved determines an efficiency criterion for each separate task. Mr N. N. Bokaryev, regards a criterion of efficiency of intellectual activity as the degree of achievement of a set aims, as well the public consciousness and psychology.

Bulgarian researcher, Georgi Byrdarov proposed the same approach, but to solve problems of propaganda efficiency: «In the most general form propa-

ganda efficiency may be determined as the overlap or full coincidence of its results with the aims and tasks set out in advance». G. Byrdarov proposes to analyze propaganda efficiency dependence on influence that it has on various fields of social life.

In his opinion, propaganda efficiency has several levels:

Fourth level—conviction growing into philosophy of life, motives of behaviour, actions

Third level—knowledge growing into convictions

Second level—mastering knowledge

First level—formation of an interest in material.

All institutions of culture in the country, without exception, were engaged in working out qualitative aspects of efficiency of the non-material sphere. The most significant research is published in «Works of S.R.I Of Culture». Among them we find the reflection results of E. I. Smirnova who proposed to determine a system of efficiency criteria of the educational work done by clubs, according to the population's participation in productive and social activities, as well as by attendance at cultural-educational events.

Attempts to systematise the existing qualitative criteria of efficiency of intellectual activities have been made by some researchers (Table № 3.5), which allow them to establish general and particular trends in building up a criteria of organization of social production in this sphere.

In consideration of the first approach in determining the efficiency of immaterial intellectual activities, one should note the absence of a specific system of criteria to estimate its planning.

Before considering the second direction one should also note that some researchers reject a wide use of quantity indicators here, but not others. On the contrary, they believe that without them it is impossible to use modern methods of planning and management. For instance, Mr. Drosdov V. A. remarked that *«quantity characteristics are of great importance, for, firstly it is efficiency that allows recording quantity changes in various characteristics of the process and its components, and secondly, it greatly facilitates formalizing an analysis apparatus. It is important in using modern means of processing social information».*

Considering the problems of quantity reflection of a cultural process, G.T. Juravlyov pays attention to an objective necessity of working out general indicators of current and long term planning: *«The workers, without waiting for scientists to solve these problems, begin to work out the indices by themselves. Thus, a level of social activity is calculated according to the formula»:*

$$C = \sqrt[8]{C_1 \cdot C_2 \cdot C_3 \cdot C_4 \cdot C_5 \cdot C_6 \cdot C_7 \cdot C_8}$$

in which C—index of the second level;
   C_1-C_8—indices of the first level, calculated by the formula:

$$C_{1-8} = \frac{C_s + C_{art} + C_{co}}{N}$$

in which
   C_1—C_8—an index of working people's participation in sport, amateur artistic work and various corporations of working people;
   C_s—number of working people attending sports sections;
   C_{art}—people taking part in amateur artistic sections;
   C_{co}—members of various working people's corporations;
   N—total number of people working.

«Examples of general indicators are given by us in order to understand the idea of a necessity in concentrating the information...Work on creating the universal indicators has not yet begun».
According to S. I. Abalkin, a system of quantity indicators of cultural-educational activities must have a structure, as follows:
   a) Indicators, characterizing the material and technical foundation of the branch;
   b) Indicators characterizing labor and financial results of the branch;
   c) Indicators characterizing organizational buildings of the branch (including so-called network indicators) and its territorial placement;
   d) Indicators characterizing results of branch activities, including the spare time assimilated by its institutions.

SYSTEMATIZING THE EXISTING QUALITATIVE CRITERIA OF IMMATERIAL-INTELLECTUAL ACTIVITIES' EFFICIENCY

Author	Number of criterion			
	1	2	3	4
S. Kosolapov,	Ideological orientation, educational value	Range of cover of the population	Club's activity outside the club	Connection with production
A. Solomonic, D. Genkin			Mass activities in club's work	Club's participation as a social organization in the social fabric
A. Sasyhov		Club's work contents		Results of educational, cultural and creative work
V. Tsukerman	Functional indicator	Mass's participation indicator	Indicator of working people's participation in club work	Indicator of sphere of influence
Connection with production	Degree of using means of mass communication	Account and education of the population's tastes	Growth of prestige and attendance	Change of personal qualities of club's audience
		Meeting interests, individually by club		
Genkin		Differentiation of club's activities by categories of population	Indicator of efficiency of using club premises, financial indicators	

We will consider the strong and weak points of each of the above groups of indicators in planning the branch «Culture».

In the first group of indicators, S. I. Abalkin includes a number of club institutions and their seats (up to 100, from 101 to 200, from 201 to 300, over
300). However, planning the development and distribution of the «Culture»
branch's fixed assets by these indicators leads to considerable disproportion,
revealed during a calculation of a the number of seats per 1000 people. We
have considered this point before.

The second group includes indicators of the branch's provision of higher education specialists, living conditions of branch workers and improvement in
their qualifications. The proposed indicators do not reflect the creation of
cultural educational services in time. That is why they cannot be taken as a
basis for planning the «Culture» branch.

In the third group of indicators S. I. Abalkin proposed a number of centralized
systems (C.S), culture complexes (C.C), a number of popular library readers. In this group of indicators «a number of C.S», «a number of C.C» are
not logically identical to «a number of popular library readers», that is why
these indicators cannot be united in one group.

In the fourth group of indicators, S. I. Abalkin proposes to use people's spare
time as assimilated by branch institutions. This is correct. However, he did
not measure these benefits by a time parameter, nor did he consider each
factor of production separately or their system of interaction. In other
words, he did not determine the economic content of «enlightenment and
entertainment service» or its economic properties. It is impossible to build a
model of this branch as well as realize its rational territorial allocation.

S. I. Abalkin proposed «*indicators, characterizing efficiency of the people's cultural
service*» as social economic indicators, in paragraph «d». However, he did
not substantiate the principles of their construction. Neither did he unite
them in a formalized form for every type of institution in the «Culture» and
«Art» branches. At the same time, a more positive aspect of his research is
some of his branch calculations.

Before considering the third direction of our research into the efficiency of cultural educational (immaterial-intellectual) activities, one should note how
positive it is that some researchers propose to determine efficiency according
to the formula: «aims-means». This idea means that our society must not
be indifferent to the kind of expenditure realized by any kind of immaterial
intellectual activity. Any other kind of activity must be calculated economically. And if expenditure exceeds results, then, naturally, the activity is not
profitable. It is pertinent to mention here J. Gilyazitdinov's point of view on
the matter. He remarked on the necessity of using the criteria, «...«enlight-
*enment and entertainment» economic profitability of expenditure spent in the
process of immaterial intellectual activities*».

Summing up the first, second and third directions of the research into the efficiency of immaterial intellectual activities, one should state that the economic peculiarities of «Culture», «Art» have not yet been revealed. This has a negative effect on the planning, development and distribution of productive forces.

DISTRIBUTION OF PRODUCTION FACTORS IN THE «THEATRE» BRANCH

For many decades planning in the «enlightenment and entertainment branches» was based on the principle «from a reached level», which did not allow a decline in the indicators of the people's cultural servicing. The disadvantage of such an approach cannot be called a principle from an economic viewpoint. It is not based on any scientific axioms. The practical utilization of the principle is witness to the fact that economic theory is absent in the development of the sphere under consideration.

The above is confirmed by the fact that an aggregate of the indicators, used in the practice of planning, reflects the development peculiarities of the «theatre» and other branches unequally, and disproportionately. Therefore if we consider an indicator such as a «attendance», then it reflects an equal volume of a consumed «service». With one film, its screening is regarded as one service (one attendee), but this heats one attendance of a 10-15 minute cartoon and of a 30 minute film as identical.

Since the «attendance» indicator reflects the amount of consumed «enlightenment and entertainment services» inadequately, then, naturally all the others, based on this component, are also reflected unequally.

The aggregate indicators below are the basis for distributing capital assets and labor resources in the theatre.

Number of performances including:
-evening ones on a stationary stage;
-guest and tour performances;
-number of spectators;
-average number of spectators per theatre;
-attendance level of occupation of the auditorium;
-attendance and accommodation of theatres per 1000 seats;
-number of new and completely re-staged performances included in a repertoire;
-performances profits;
-theatre expenses on exploitation;
-average income per performance;

-average takings from performances per spectator;
-average number of spectators per performance;
-average theatre expenses per performance;
-size of staff in the main activities, including actors, artistic directors;
-wages fund.

This combination of indicators reflects the negative essence of the branch distribution mechanism: placement, use of fixed capital, financial resources, labor forces as well as the «theatre branch» services in time and space.

From the above it is clear that none of the indicators or their total combination can adequately reflect the dialectics of the «theatre branch» development. They do not allow us either to determine a real state of affairs in the branch or to work out a distinct, long-term strategy for its development. The problem lies in the politico-economic foundation of the criteria that reflect the processes of the «theatre branch».

A part from the basis of long-term plans, rates of population increment were not taken into account. This has led to a considerable disproportional development of the «enlightenment and entertainment branches»—from a material and technical basis. For instance, the differing in a level of museum provision was 31.2 times (See table № 3.6).

DIFFERENTIATION BETWEEN THE REPUBLICS IN PROVISION OF CULTURE INSTITUTIONS
(PER 1000 PEOPLE)

Culture Institutions And Kinds of Service	1	10	20	24
Theatre	5.6	4.8	3.6	3.6
Music collectives	9.2	10.6	7.0	7.7
Stationary circuses	N/A	5.4	6.7	6.5
Museum (all departments including art museums)	15.2 / 17.0	18.2 / 9.8	19.6 / 12.0	21.0 / 31.2
Library (all department universal and popular of all and book funds)	3.3	2.7	2.9	3.1
Club institution (all departments)	2.1	2.3	2.7	2.6
Cinemas	2.1	2.6	2.5	2.7

Reproaches against the existing aggregate of indicators can be heard every-where. For instance, J. Kapelush remarks on a disastrous situation in the statistics of concert activities: «*We have neither a sociological nor statistical picture here. How many, for example, piano concerts were held in concert halls in any city and how can such concerts be commensurable with those of rock groups and their fans and spectators?*

Organs of management and institutions of culture need information about the real participation of various groups of people in the cultural process. They need to know constantly, so to say, the «temperature» of this process. Otherwise, dis-tortions in branch planning are inevitable. It is obvious».

Professors U. Fok-Babushkin, B. Rubinstein and V. Naygoldberg explain the existing problems as follows: «*It may seem at first sight that this is the matter of stable cultural traditions, that in some regions some kinds of art institutions have already existed for a long time while in others they have just appeared. It is partially true, of course. One cannot explain why changes in differentia-tion appear so suddenly in separate periods, when some coming together of a cultural situation is changed for distinct differences (for example, concert attendance). The main reason for the existing differences is the great difference of opportunities for attending cultural institutions for inhabitants of different regions, which is explained by the different provision in these institutions. This situation has come about mainly because a program and aim method of plan-ning has not been applied until recently. There was no scientific assessment of each republic's needs for various kinds of cultural institutions. Planning based on the principle «from an achieved level» could not fulfill these tasks on level-ing unmotivated territorial differences*».[35]

«As table № 3.7 reveals, the differences between republics' provision for muse-ums and book funds have increased considerably over the last decades; as for the other types of «Culture» institutions, the differences have remained either stable or decreased slightly».

The paradox of this situation is that all these professors and their institutes have distortedly «planned» the development of the «Culture» and «Art» branches, and only then have they established «*general trends of processes occurring over a long enough period*».

---

35 «Methodological problems of long term planning of artistic culture develop-ment» (Collection of articles), M.

DIFFERENTIATION IN ATTENDANCE OF CULTURE INSTITUTIONS
(PER 1000 PEOPLE IN THE POPULATION)

Culture Institutions And Kinds of Service	1	10	20	24
Theatres	4.7	3.8	3.9	3.8
Concerts	4.7	6.5	5.6	6.2
Stationary circus	N/A.	5.3	14.1	4.1
Museums of all categories including:	9.0	12.9	15.1	13.9
Art museums	12.0	36.9	58.0	46.3
Universal and popular libraries of C.M system				
Books	4.0	4.4	4.2	3.8
Number of readers	3.0	3.3	2.7	2.4
Club institutions of C.M. system group members	N/A.	18.0	8.3	4.9
Amateur performance and concert attendance	N/A	6.1	4.5	5.8
Movie showing	2.1	2.0	2.0	1.8

The Ministry of Culture and the Institute of Economy conducted complex research to determine the current and prospective attendance of culture institutions from a social and regional point of view to work out «a long term plan of improvement of the people's service». They questioned experts, mostly employees of regional, city and district cultural departments. But the research was conducted in a rather bad way. The multi-paged questionnaires were only 50 per cent filled in. The Central economic-mathematical institute did a great amount of work «editing» the bulk of information, applying correlation and other methods. But the low quality of collected information on current and prospective attendance, naturally affected drawing up of «long-term plans of culture development». For instance, they paid no attention to the material and technical problems in the development of a network of children's theaters. There were seven times fewer puppet theaters than the norm and theatres four times fewer for young spectators.

It is interesting to see how the Ministry of Culture used to consider the problems of long-term planning to develop the «enlightenment and entertainment branches». Order № 297 at the Ministry of Culture noted that it was particularly necessary to develop:

Branch schemes of cultural development and distribution, which serve the people. They include:

I. Theatre and entertainment enterprise development schemes.
  1.1. Network of professional theatres.
  1.2. Network of concert halls.
  1.3. Network of large philharmonic collectives.
  1.4. Network of circuses.

II. Culture and education institutions' development and distribution schemes.
  2.1. Network of club institutions (by types).
  2.2. Network of popular and universal libraries.
  2.3. Network of culture and recreation parks.
  2.4. Network of zoo's.
  2.5. Network of museums.
  2.6. Network of exhibition halls.

III. Education institution development and distribution schemes.
  3.1. Network of the higher institutes of the Ministry of Culture.
  3.2. Network of vocational institutions.
  3.3. Network of children's music, artistic, choreographic schools, art schools.

IV. Scheme of development and distribution of industry enterprises, producing cultural equipment.

V. Scheme of development and distribution of the enterprises producing records, compact discs, cassettes and videos.

VI. Scheme of development and distribution of organizations restoring architecture as historical and cultural monuments.

VII. Schemes of development and distribution of organizations, installing theatre equipment in the country.

Long-term planning, building the «enlightenment and entertainment branches» distribution and development schemes are rather complicated because its many economical problems have not been worked out so far. In particular, there is no criterion to determine the socio-economic efficiency of the considered branches' enterprise resources.

Rational or irrational functioning of entertainment and music institutions depends on whether we can find an optimal version, in time and space of their development and placement at the zero stage. The question is motivated by the fact that society is not indifferent the expenditure on the «enlightenment and entertainment branch» and the results the considered branch of the national economy will achieve in the future.

Planning of «enlightenment and entertainment branch» undoubtedly takes into account indicators that characterize time and spatial distribution of fixed assets and its labor forces all over cities, regions and the country as a whole. The quality of planning considerably depends on these inherent and logical indicators. If there are no system indicators, or they lack logic, errors are inevitable.

CHAPTER 9

VERTICAL ASPECT OF «ENLIGHTENMENT AND ENTERTAINMENT» MARKET

To a certain degree, the horizontal study of «enlightenment and entertainment» market was revealed in the previous chapter that absolute indicators do not take into account expenses that are necessary for any structure of the populations' spare time budget. We will try to eradicate that obvious defect in the present chapter.

What do we mean be vertical aspect of the population's spare time resource (STP)? First of all, people's spare time expenses must be boxed into relative criteria. Such criteria are necessary because the population's spare time activities may vary from year to year. Without this we may unintentionally omit the size of the population inhabiting any territory, their potential spare time resource, rate of growth, and the expenses spent on the development of the STP resource. That «everything is fine» in some cities and regions may turn into a critical situation in the «enlightenment and entertainment branches». Therefore a horizontal study of the «enlightenment and entertainment» market must be complemented by a vertical study, the essence of which will be considered below.

The main requirements of social and economic criteria in the «enlightenment and entertainment branches» are as follows:

♦ aim indicators of an individual «enlightenment and entertainment» enterprise, a group, and the branch as a whole must, as much as possible, characterize the results of their work and their contribution to a common result—a non material product;

♦   economic criteria must reflect the level of organization of an indi-
    vidual enterprise and a group of «enlightenment and entertainment
    branches» in retrospect, current and prospective consideration;
♦   the system of criteria must be substantiated and optimized by theory;
♦   the criteria must be based on the principle of economic efficiency—
    achievement of maximum results with minimum expenses (according to
    the essence of the formula «results-expenses», or «expenses-results»;
♦   the criteria must be of the same type and quantitatively determined.

One must understand that an economic efficiency criterion should: reflect both
particular and general aspects of organization. In this case an individual
enterprise and a group of enterprises in the «enlightenment and entertainment branches» have correlation of its external functions with an expenses
function.
In general form it may appear as follows:

$$C = \frac{\text{results}}{\text{expenditures}}$$

Since labor expenses are is ambivalent by nature and given that expenses are
equal to the expenses of direct labor plus the cost of past labor, a general
system of economic efficiency criteria can be recorded as follows:

$$Ce = \begin{cases} C1 = \dfrac{\text{results}}{\text{expenses of past labor}} \; ; \\[2em] C2 = \dfrac{\text{results}}{\text{expenses of direct labor}} \; ; \\[2em] C3 = \dfrac{\text{results}}{\text{aggregate expenses}} \; ; \end{cases}$$

The criteria **C1, C2, C3** are identical. They are based on the uniform logic of construction.

If a branch's activity results appear, as a developed STP resource, then compression of this specific result with the expenses allows us to construct a system of criteria of «enlightenment and entertainment branch» efficiency.

Within the «enlightenment and entertainment branch» framework «results and expenses» reflect the connection between an inner function of socializing the population's activities during their spare time and an internal function of expenses.

From this it follows that economic efficiency of «enlightenment and entertainment branches» development should be written as follows:

$$
Ks = \begin{cases}
1.\ \text{Criterion «thesis»} = \dfrac{V}{\text{branch expenses of past labor}}\ ; \\[3ex]
2.\ \text{Criterion «antithesis»}\ B = \dfrac{V}{\text{branch expenses of direct labor}}\ ; \\[3ex]
3.\ \text{Criterion «thesis»}\quad C = \dfrac{V}{\text{aggregate branch expenses}}\ ;
\end{cases}
$$

where V—assimilated resource of population spare time (STP) by «enlightenment and entertainment branches».

The proposed system of socio-economic efficiency criteria reflects both a general (branch) and individual aspect. This system appears as an individual one by dividing the volume of branch services by the combined expenses of past, direct and assimilated labor. Then we get individual values for each of these criteria.

A. A SYSTEM OF CRITERIA OF RESOURCES UTILISED IN THE «ENLIGHTENMENT AND ENTERTAINMENT BRANCHES»

I. Criteria efficiency system in units of time measurement on the basis of a reverse criterion:

$$\text{a) } F = \frac{\text{Result—developed resource of } A_{STP} \text{ (man—hour)}}{\text{Past labor expenses in units of cost measurement}}$$

$$\text{b) } P = \frac{\text{Result—developed resource of } A_{STP} \text{ (man—hour)}}{\text{Direct labor expenses in units of cost measurement}}$$

$$\text{c) } C = \frac{\text{Result—developed resource of } A_{STP} \text{ (man—hour)}}{\text{Aggregate labor expenses in units of cost measurement}}$$

II. Criteria efficiency system in cost units of measurement on the basis of a resource criterion:

$$\text{a) } F = \frac{\text{Result (estimated cost of developed resource of } A_{STP})}{\text{Past labor expenses in units of cost measurement}}$$

$$\text{b) } P = \frac{\text{Result (estimated cost of developed resource of } A_{STP})}{\text{Direct labor expenses in units of cost measurement}}$$

$$\text{c) } C = \frac{\text{Result (estimated cost of developed resource of } A_{STP})}{\text{Aggregate labor expenses in units of cost measurement}}$$

III. Synthesized system of efficiency criteria:

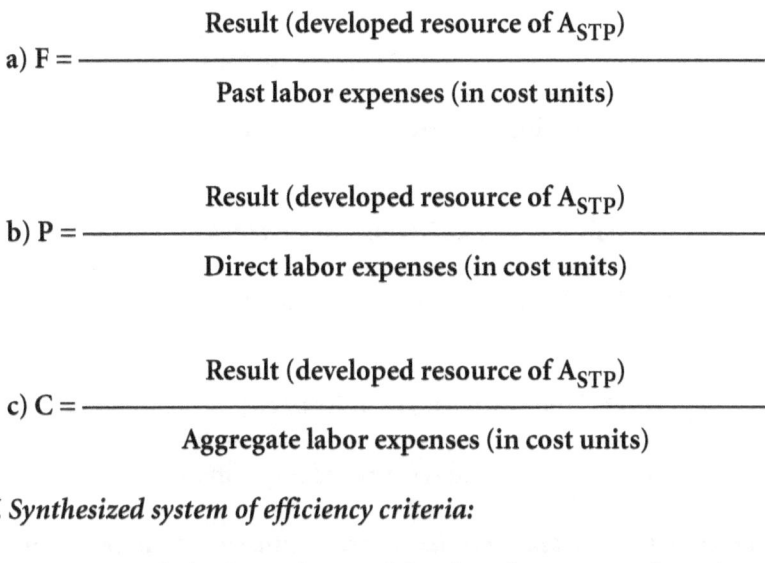

$$\text{a) } F = \frac{\text{Result (developed resource of } A_{STP})}{\text{Past labor expenses (in cost units)}}$$

$$\text{b) } P = \frac{\text{Result (developed resource of } A_{STP})}{\text{Direct labor expenses (in cost units)}}$$

$$\text{c) } C = \frac{\text{Result (developed resource of } A_{STP})}{\text{Aggregate labor expenses (in cost units)}}$$

IV. Synthesized system of efficiency criteria:

$$\text{a) } F = \frac{\text{Result (estimated cost of developed resource of } A_{STP})}{\text{Past labor expenses in units of cost measurement}}$$

$$\text{b) } P = \frac{\text{Result (estimated cost of developed resource of } A_{STP})}{\text{Direct labor expenses in units of cost measurement}}$$

$$\text{c) } C = \frac{\text{Result (estimated cost of developed resource of } A_{STP})}{\text{Aggregate labor expenses in units of cost measurement}}$$

I a. Efficiency criteria system in units of time measurement (on the basis of a direct criterion): [36]

$$\text{a) } F^{-1} = \frac{\text{Past labor expenses in units of cost measurement}}{\text{Result—developed resource of } A_{STP} \text{ (man-hour)}}$$

$$\text{b) } P^{-1} = \frac{\text{Direct labor expenses in units of cost measurement}}{\text{Result—developed resource of } A_{STP} \text{ (man-hour)}}$$

$$\text{c) } C^{-1} = \frac{\text{Aggregate labor expenses in units of cost measurement}}{\text{Result—developed resource of } A_{STP} \text{ (man-hour)}}$$

II a. Efficiency criteria system in units of cost measurement (on the basis of a direct criterion):

$$\text{a) } F^{-1} = \frac{\text{Past labor expenses in units of cost measurement}}{\text{Result (estimated cost of developed resource of } A_{STP})}$$

$$\text{b) } P^{-1} = \frac{\text{Direct labor expenses in units of cost measurement}}{\text{Result (estimated cost of developed resource of } A_{STP})}$$

$$\text{c) } C^{-1} = \frac{\text{Aggregate labor expenses in units of cost measurement}}{\text{Result (estimated cost of developed resource of } A_{STP})}$$

---

36 I Variant A_{STP} -assimilated resource of population spare time

II Variant $m + A_{STP}$ -income and assimilated resource of population spare time

III Variant $v + m + A_{STP}$ -wages, income and assimilated resource of population spare time

III a. Synthesized system of efficiency criteria:

a) $F^{-1} = \dfrac{\text{Past labor expenses (in units of cost)}}{\text{Result (developed resource of } A_{STP})}$

b) $P^{-1} = \dfrac{\text{Direct labor expenses (in units of cost)}}{\text{Result (developed resource of } A_{STP})}$

c) $C^{-1} = \dfrac{\text{Aggregate labor expenses (in units of cost)}}{\text{Result (developed resource of } A_{STP})}$

IV a. Synthesized system of efficiency criteria:

a) $F^{-1} = \dfrac{\text{Past labor expenses (in units of time)}}{\text{Result (estimated cost of developed resource of } A_{STP})}$

b) $P^{-1} = \dfrac{\text{Direct labor expenses (in units of time)}}{\text{Result (estimated cost of developed resource of } A_{STP})}$

c) $C^{-1} = \dfrac{\text{Aggregate labor expenses (in units of time)}}{\text{Result (estimated cost of developed resource of } A_{STP})}$

B. FORMALIZED FORM OF SYSTEM CRITERIA EFFICIENCY OF USING RESOURCES IN THE «ENLIGHTENMENT AND ENTERTAINMENT BRANCHES»

In order to estimate the formalized criteria for using «enlightenment and entertainment branches» resources one should emphasize that institutions in this branches have internal and external systems of development. Its external function is maximum production of «enlightenment and entertainment services» directed to satisfy the intellectual needs of the population. Its internal function is the expense of labor necessary to produce these specific services. The larger the developed STP resource with smaller expenses, the higher the efficiency of using this branch's resources and vice versa.

REGIONAL SOCIO-ECONOMIC EFFICIENCY OF USING PAST LABOR IN «ENLIGHTENMENT AND ENTERTAINMENT BRANCHES»

I. Regional fixed asset productivity of the theatre (concert organizations)

$$E_{PL}^T = \frac{\sum\limits_{j=1}^{m}\sum\limits_{i=1}^{n}\left(V_{ij}^c + V_{ij}^n\right)}{\sum\limits_{j=1}^{m}\left(PL_j^c + PL_j^n\right)}$$

where

V_{ij}^c, V_{ij}^n —assimilation A_{STP} fixed and variable forms of service in j-theatre respectively;

PL_j^c, PL_j^n —cost of material balance (past labor)—technical basis of a j-theatre institution with fixed and variable services;

i —nomenclature of services produced by theatre;

j —number of theatre institutions in a region.

II. Regional fixed asset productivity of circus (entertainment) enterprises

$$E_{PL}^{C} = \frac{\sum\limits_{j=1}^{m}\sum\limits_{i=1}^{n}\left(C_{ij}^{c} + C_{ij}^{n}\right)}{\sum\limits_{j=1}^{m}\left(PL_{j}^{c} + PL_{j}^{n}\right)}$$

where

C_{ij}^{c}, C_{ij}^{n}	-assimilation resource A_{STP};
PL_{j}^{c}, PL_{j}^{n}	-cost of material balance (past labor)—technical basis of j-circus (entertainment) institutions;
$i = n,\dots 1$	-nomenclature of non-material benefits, produced by the circus;
$j = m,\dots p$	-number of circus enterprises in a region.

III. Regional fixed asset productivity of cinemas
where

$$E_{PL}^{C} = \frac{\sum\limits_{j=1}^{m}\sum\limits_{i=1}^{n}\left(C_{ij}^{c} + C_{ij}^{n}\right)}{\sum\limits_{j=1}^{m}\left(PL_{j}^{c} + PL_{j}^{n}\right)}$$

C_{ij}^{c}, C_{ij}^{n}	-assimilation resource A_{STP} (on a i-film in a j-cinema in a given region);
PL_{j}^{c}, PL_{j}^{n}	-cost of active and passive articles of j-cinemas in a region;
i	-number of films screened;
j	-number of cinemas in a region.

IV. Regional fixed asset productivity of «Television» («Broadcasting») activities

$$E_P^P = \frac{\sum_{l=1}^{p}\sum_{j=1}^{m}\sum_{i=1}^{n} T_{ijl}}{\sum_{j=1}^{m}\left(\mathrm{PL}_j^c + \sum_{l=1}^{p}\mathrm{BC}1\right)}$$

where

Tij   -volume of production services «TV Broadcasting» on a i-transmission, in a j-social-demographic group in l-region;

-cost of fixed costs of television stations (radio stations), re-transmitting installations in l-region.

REGIONAL SOCIAL ECONOMIC EFFICIENCY OF USING DIRECT LABOR IN «ENLIGHTENMENT AND ENTERTAINMENT BRANCHES»

I. Criterion of socio-economic efficiency of using direct labor forces in the theatre (concert)

$$E_{LL}^T = \frac{\sum_{j=1}^{m}\sum_{i=1}^{n}\left(V_{ij}^c + V_{ij}^n\right)}{\sum_{j=1}^{m}\left(LL_j^c + LL_j^n\right)}$$

where
value of V_{ij}^c, V_{ij}^n -assimilated resource A_{STP};

LL_j^c, LL_j^n -direct labor expenses in the preparation and production of «enlightenment and entertainment services» in j-theatre (concert) of a region with fixed and variable services;

i   -nomenclature of «enlightenment and entertainment services», produced by theatre institution in a region;

j   -number of theatre in a region.

II. Socio-economic efficiency of using direct labor in circus enterprises (entertainment)

$$E_{LL}^{\text{Ц}} = \frac{\sum\limits_{j=1}^{m}\sum\limits_{i=1}^{n}\left(C_{ij}^{c} + C_{ij}^{n}\right)}{\sum\limits_{j=1}^{m}\left(LL_{j}^{c} + LL_{j}^{n}\right)}$$

where

values C_{ij}^{c}, C_{ij}^{n}	-assimilated resource A_{STP};
LL_{j}^{c}, LL_{j}^{n}-	direct labor expenses on i-technology with fixed and variable services;
i	-nomenclature of intellectual benefits produced by circus enterprises in a region;
j	-number of circus (entertainment).

III. Socio-economic efficiency of using direct labor in cinemas

$$E_{LL}^{C} = \frac{\sum\limits_{j=1}^{m}\sum\limits_{i=1}^{n}\left(C_{ij}^{c} + C_{ij}^{n}\right)}{\sum\limits_{j=1}^{m}\left(LL_{j}^{c} + LL_{j}^{n}\right)}$$

where
values of C_{ij}^{c}, C_{ij}^{n} -assimilated resource A_{STP};

LL_{j}^{c}, LL_{j}^{n}	-expenses of direct labor in a j-cinema of a region;
i	-number of films;
j	-number of cinemas in a region.

IV. Socio-economic efficiency of using direct labor in «Television» and «Broadcasting»

$$E_{LL}^{P} = \frac{\sum\limits_{l=1}^{p}\sum\limits_{j=1}^{m}\sum\limits_{i=1}^{n} T_{ijl}}{\sum\limits_{i=1}^{n} LL_i}$$

where

T_{ijl} -assimilated resource ASTP;

LL_i -expenses of direct labor in production of i-benefit-services in l-region.

REGIONAL SOCIAL ECONOMIC EFFICIENCY OF USING AGGREGATE LABOR IN «ENLIGHTENMENT AND ENTERTAINMENT BRANCHES»

I. Aggregate regional socio-economic efficiency of theatre (concert) activities

$$E_C^T = \frac{\sum\limits_{j=1}^{m}\sum\limits_{i=1}^{n}\left(V_{ij}^c + V_{ij}^n\right)}{\sum\limits_{j=1}^{m}\left(I_j^c + I_j^n\right)}$$

where

values, V_{ij}^c, V_{ij}^n -assimilated resource A_{STP};

I_j^c, I_j^n -cost of production of «enlightenment and entertainment» benefits in j-theatre institutions in a region with fixed and variable services;

i   -nomenclature of «enlightenment and entertainment» benefits produced by theatres;

j   -number of theatre (concert) institutions in a region.

II. Aggregate regional socio-economic efficiency of circus (entertainment) enterprises' activities

$$E_C^C = \frac{\displaystyle\sum_{j=1}^{m}\sum_{i=1}^{n}\left(\mathbf{C}_{ij}^c + \mathbf{C}_{ij}^n\right)}{\displaystyle\sum_{j=1}^{m}\left(\mathbf{I}_j^c + \mathbf{I}_j^n\right)}$$

where
values $\mathbf{C}_{ij}^c, \mathbf{C}_{ij}^n$ — -assimilated resource A_{STP};

$\mathbf{I}_j^c, \mathbf{I}_j^n$ -costs of production of «enlightenment and entertainment» benefits in j-mobile form of service respectively;

i   -nomenclature of «enlightenment and entertainment» benefits produced by circus enterprises;

j   -number of circus in a region.

III. Aggregate regional socio-economic efficiency of cinemas activities

$$E_C^C = \frac{\displaystyle\sum_{j=1}^{m}\sum_{i=1}^{n}\left(\mathbf{C}_{ij}^c + \mathbf{C}_{ij}^n\right)}{\displaystyle\sum_{j=1}^{m}\left(\mathbf{I}_j^c + \mathbf{I}_j^n\right)}$$

where
values $\mathbf{C}_{ij}^c, \mathbf{C}_{ij}^n$ — -assimilated resource A_{STP} resource of people's spare time spent on i-film in a j-cinema in a region;

$\mathbf{I}_j^c, \mathbf{I}_j^n$ -total costs of serving the population in a j-cinema, in a region;

i   -number of films;

j   -number of cinemas in a region.

IV. Collective regional socio-economic efficiency of «TV Broadcasting» activities

$$E_C^R = \frac{\sum_{l=1}^{p}\sum_{j=1}^{m}\sum_{i=1}^{n} T_{ijl}}{\sum_{i=1}^{n} I_i}$$

where

T_{ijl} -assimilated resource ASTP of «TV Broadcasting»;

I_i -total cost of production of television and radio services.

CHAPTER 10

ECONOMIC PROPERTIES OF THE «ENLIGHTENMENT AND ENTERTAINMENT BRANCHES»

«While working in the regional financial department in 1976, I found out that geometrical figures like triangles, squares and rhombi of different colors come out as indicators for the activities of the «Culture» and «Art» branches. The first thing I thought about was the refinement and inventiveness of the human mind. How can one deem the intellectual services to be shown with the geometrical figures?»

A. ECONOMIC PROPERTIES OF THE «ENLIGHTENMENT AND ENTERTAINMENT SERVICE»

Determination of the essence of the «intellectual value» category is the primordial point. It is not possible to begin the evaluation of results of labor in the intellectual sphere without this category. It is possible to consider an inner economic content provided the general contours are formed for the category.

If we consider the existing aggregate of the intellectual values, they can be divided into two groups:

-<u>The First group</u>—the intellectual values that have materialized into a subject, a thing; for example, a book, a picture, a film, a score, etc (we can call them material-intellectual values);

-<u>The Second group</u>—the intellectual values that have not materialized into a subject or a thing. They are consumed while in the process of their creation, while treating people with some specific means and instruments of labor of the intellectual sphere at a unit of time (we call them immaterial-intellectual services).

The intellectual values and intellectual services are organically interconnected and they form their unique aggregate. Thus, for instance, a lack of film reel (that comes out as an intellectual value in the given case) does not allow production of intellectual services of cinema art. It should be noted that an intellectual service appears in the case when human labor is spent—labor of an actor, of a musician, of a teacher. There is no consumption of the intellectual services without their production, or vice versa.

Based upon the above, we can draft the following dialectical scheme:

DIALECTIC SCHEME OF A SOLITARY INTELLECTUAL PRODUCT

Thesis   Solitary intellectual value

Antithesis   Solitary intellectual service

Synthesis   Solitary (aggregate) intellectual product (intellectual value and intellectual service)

USAGE VALUE OF THE «ENLIGHTENMENT AND ENTERTAINMENT SERVICE»

«The first question that arises while getting to know the economic properties of the intellectual services is: Does a service of culture, art, church, film distribution, TV and Radio Broadcasting come out as a commodity?»

A «enlightenment and entertainment service» comes out as a commodity provided it is a product of labor for the others. It is one thing if you play the Tchiakovsky First Concert of for yourself, and another if the concert is

played for an audience in a hall. The proposed «enlightenment and entertainment service» does not come out as a social use value in the first case,
but it becomes one in the second.

The use value of a «enlightenment and entertainment service» as a result of the
operation of the concrete labor of a dancer, a singer, a musician or an actor,
is the result of action and motion of specific factors of the labor process:
-means of labor;
-instruments of labor;
-subject of labor (persons);
-employees of the «enlightenment and entertainment branches» (a dancer,
a singer, a musician, etc.).

A solitary service, for instance, or «a mono-service» (a mono-product) of the
«enlightenment and entertainment branches» is the result of the directed
action of a solitary-aggregate employee on to a solitary-aggregate subject
of labor (an individual), using solitary means and instruments of labor at a
time unit. The solitary services are different in their content and form within
the frames of each of the «enlightenment and entertainment branches».

The enterprises of the «enlightenment and entertainment branches» create
the variety of relevant services for the people. The services are different in
their structure and have a multi-functional purpose. They must meet any
segment of human intellectual needs. This is the only condition when a
«enlightenment and entertainment service» is purchased or consumed.[37] It
comes out as such only in the process of its consumption by people.

Any change in the structures of people's intellectual needs determinedly influences a co-relation of the «enlightenment and entertainment services» in
their whole aggregate. Not all of them keep their attractiveness. As regards
this branch, an influence of fashion causes loss of interest towards one and
increase of interest towards another.

There are some deviations between «a function of demand» and «a function
of supply» of these services in the considered branch, where a production
phase coincides with the consumption phase of the «enlightenment and
entertainment services». Thus, for instance, a «function of supply» is two

---

[37] The use value of a «enlightenment and entertainment service» as a product of
human labor does not depend on whether it is created in terms of a private, state or
mixed property of the production means. The aggregate of the «enlightenment and
entertainment services» can be divided into types, kinds and families: theatre, circus,
show, cinema, etc.

times higher than a «function of demand» in the half empty theatres, concert halls and cinemas.

VALUE OF THE «ENLIGHTENMENT AND ENTERTAINMENT SERVICE»

If we consider the «enlightenment and entertainment services» as a commodity, it should be noted that it is very difficult to set up their dual nature, as the services are immaterial. Nevertheless, the following conclusions are quite clear:

-First, expenses of the past and direct labor connected with creating the «enlightenment and entertainment services»;

-Second, the labor expenses accumulated in the «enlightenment and entertainment service» stem as general labor expenses (in the frames of the socially arranged process of production);

-Third, the labor of the «enlightenment and entertainment service» creators is dual by its nature. It is concrete and a source of use value, and, on the other hand, it comes out as a source of commodity cost.

It is to a larger extend the intellectual energy of the enterprises' employees and to a lesser extend a physical one that is spent while creating the «enlightenment and entertainment services» in the theatres, concert halls, circuses, church institutions, and TV and Radio broadcasting. The labor expenses of the people of art and culture (as such) do not differ from the labor expenses of the people, who create the material values. These expenses are identical. A simple formula is possible here:

Expenses of intellectual and physical power during production of the «enlightenment and entertainment services	=	Expenses of physical and intellectual power while during production of material values

It follows from the above simple equality that the «enlightenment and entertainment services», like the material values, accumulate a homogeneous human labor, which reveals itself only when there is an exchange of intellectual services for other services and commodities.

If the intellectual services do not carry any cost (that is, labor expenses on their creation do not come out as a part of the social labor expenses), then they cannot be exchanged for other commodities and services. This is the reason why the motion of the resource streaming into the intellectual sphere is violated. The same would lead to a distortion in the entire economy.

A negation of the homogeneous labor in the intellectual services by a lot of political economists generated a well-known «residual principle» of directing the means for development of the intellectual sphere. It is possible to leave the principle provided we accept the show, emotional and informational services to accumulate homogeneous labor and to bear some cost relations. Thus, an exchange mechanism between the intellectual and other spheres of social production works in this case.

EXCHANGE VALUE OF THE «ENLIGHTENMENT AND ENTERTAINMENT SERVICE»

Political economists understand an exchange value as the ability of one commodity to be exchanged for other commodities in some definite proportion. If we apply the same to a «enlightenment and entertainment service», the question arises: What is the basis for its exchange for other commodities and services? The question is possible to be answered as follows:

If we consider intellectual services and material values as the use values, they are different and cannot be quantitatively measured. The usefulness of a singer's services and the usefulness of bread are oriented to meet people's different needs. The bread cannot replace the services of a singer or vice versa. But as production expenses are incurred in the first and second case, bread and the services of a singer are homogeneous as per this (expense) indication. Therefore, they can be exchanged in a definite proportion.

Thus, we can see that labor when creating the «enlightenment and entertainment services» is dual in nature. Such an interconnection is possible to be schematically written down as follows:

DUAL CHARACTER OF LABOR ENCLOSED IN A ENLIGHTENMENT AND ENTERTAINMENT SERVICE»

Thesis   Concrete labor process on creating a «enlightenment and entertainment service».

Antithesis Homogeneous labor process on creating a «enlightenment and entertainment service».

Synthesis   Process of creating a «enlightenment and entertainment service» as such. (Concrete labor process and homogeneous labor process)

If we assume 10 «enlightenment and entertainment services» can be theoretically exchanged for other commodities and services in the following proportion:

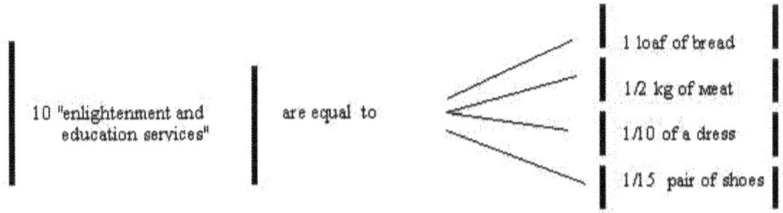

The exchange relations reveal that an equal quantity of human labor is enclosed in a «enlightenment and entertainment service» and bread. This proportion can be changed depending on the quality of the «enlightenment and entertainment services». If the dance group of Moiseev gives a show, these are services of one quality, and the «enlightenment and entertainment services» of some district dance group are of another quality.

The exchange relations that exist between the «enlightenment and entertainment services» and other commodities and services characterize the fact of abstraction of the material and immaterial concrete forms. The proportion, which they are exchanged in, determines a quantity of the homogeneous labor that is enclosed in a «enlightenment and entertainment service».

Acceptance of the labor of a dancer, a singer and a musician, as a source of the intellectual welfare leads to the conclusion that it comes out as a source of the exchange value in its definite specific form. The above stated enables us to write the following structure.

DUAL STRUCTURE OF ECONOMIC PROPERTIES OF A «ENLIGHTENMENT AND ENTERTAINMENT SERVICE»

Thesis   Use value of a «enlightenment and entertainment service»

Antithesis   Value of a «enlightenment and entertainment service»

Synthesis   Exchange value of a «enlightenment and entertainment service»

SUBJECTIVE EVALUATION OF VALUE OF THE «ENLIGHTENMENT AND ENTERTAINMENT SERVICES»

It is possible to measure a value of «enlightenment and entertainment service» in several ways. One of them is a sociological questionnaire. Thus, if only one visitor defines the cost to attend a museum, it would be a subjective evaluation. And if 1000 or 3000 people participate in the same, the degree of the subjective character is considerably decreased and the evaluation obtains an objective character.

STRUCTURE OF SUBJECTIVE ESTIMATION OF THE COST OF A TICKET IN THE ART MUSEUM

Index Name	Specific gravity, in %	Ticket cost, in %									
		Free of charge	10 cent.	20 cent.	30 cent.	40 cent.	50 cent.	60 cent.	70 cent.	80 cent.	more than 1 dollar
Total, including	100	5,9	3,6	30	11,8	7,4	19	4	1,8	2,7	9,8
Odessa's visitors :	20	4	6	34	3	9	17	4	2	3	9
	80	7	3	29	12	8	21	5	2	3	11
By sex,	93										
men:	35	7	5	28	12	7	21	5	1	2	10
women:	58	5	3	31	13	8	20	4	2	3	10
Structure of subjective ticket price for children		38	40	11,2	3	1	2,2	0,5	0,5	0,5	

A questionnaire of the visitors of the Art museum allows setting up the following:
-Only 5,9 per cent of the visitors want a free of charge attendance of the museum;
-56,6 per cent of the visitors asked believe that the price of the tickets for adults should be increased.

Sorting of the sociological information made it possible to determine a structure of subjective ticket prices for children (up to 12 years old): 38 per cent of those interviewed consider that children should visit the museum free of charge. Almost half of the visitors suggested to fix the ticket price at 10 cents, and only 19 per cent of the interviewed visitors thought it was necessary to increase the entry fee for children slightly.

LIBRARIES

The personnel of regional libraries in addition to their main function offer the population the following services:
-drawing up «brief» and «detailed» references on the matters interesting to readers;
-text copying;
-foreign language translations;
-«porch-to-porch» literature delivery

At present, universal scientific library personnel render free services to the population in the form of «brief» and «detailed» references on the subjects, which interest readers. Such references are widely used by postgraduate students, scientific workers, scholars and management staff.
While making a sociological research in the libraries, we put some questions, answers to which may substantiate a cost for some services. After sorting out the information contained in 644 questionnaires we found that this group of questions was answered by nearly 58,4 per cent of the interviewed persons.
Analysis of the given data shows that drawing up a «brief» reference could be profitable for librarians.
One of the promising trends in library activity could also be such specific service as «porch-to-porch» literature delivery. Thus, surveying of visitors of the universal scientific library resulted in the following:

SUBJECTIVE COST ESTIMATION OF «BRIEF REFERENCE» SERVICE
(in percentage of responded)

Hypothetical cost of service	Drawing up of a «brief» reference			
	10 books review	20 books review	30 books review	
50 cents				
1 dollars	50	3,7		
2 dollars	29		9	
3 dollars	9			
4 dollars	10	50,6		
5 dollars	2			
6 dollars		33,4		
7 dollars				
8 dollars		6,5	53	
9 dollars				
10 dollars		5,8	16	
12 dollars			17	
15 dollars			5	

ECONOMIC STRUCTURE OF THE «ENLIGHTENMENT AND ENTERTAINMENT SERVICE»

The crucial problems related to the organization and planning of «enlightenment and entertainment» enterprises work consist of the following: can results of activity of a museum staff, a concert enterprise or a library be calculated for a quarter, six month or a year? Is it possible to automatically transfer calculation formulas used in material production to «enlightenment and entertainment branches»?

I presume that economic evaluation of «enlightenment and entertainment» enterprises activity can be and should be carried out with the same accuracy and sequence of calculations applied in any other sector of the national economy. Value of «enlightenment and entertainment service» and any other commodity should be calculated by the following formula:

$$C + V + M = P,$$

where
   C is depreciation, transferred part of capital funds value (of past labor);
   V is wages;
   M is a surplus product

Ratio of these three items between each other may be different:
   -1st version C = const, V and M are variables
   -2nd version V = const, C and M are variables
   -3rd version M = const, C and V are variables
   -4th version C, V = const, M is variable and so on.

Here we will consider peculiarities of this formula in some sub-branches of the «enlightenment and entertainment sphere».

MUSEUM INSTITUTIONS

During the operation of a museum institution, building ware and tear, communications and material and intellectual values (paintings, sculptures etc.) progresses at different «rates». For example, communications deteriorate within 15-25 years but the building itself can stand for a hundred years. That is why depreciation deductions are also different: for a building it is two to three per cent annually; communications it is six to 10 per cent annually. These depreciation deductions should be regarded as part of the museum services value.

It is more or less clear with the museums' capital funds. But how can one estimate the amount of depreciation of the active part of a museum—material and intellectual values—paintings, sculptures? Cost of the latter increases from year to year and the condition of paintings differs a lot. This is why depreciation charges cannot be a fixed value; they should change depending on the value of a work of art. I think that the amount of depreciation for the active part of the museum's capital funds should be directly matched with the condition of the works of art. The worse the conditions of paintings storage are, the greater amount of means for their restoration should be. This situation can be represented graphically:

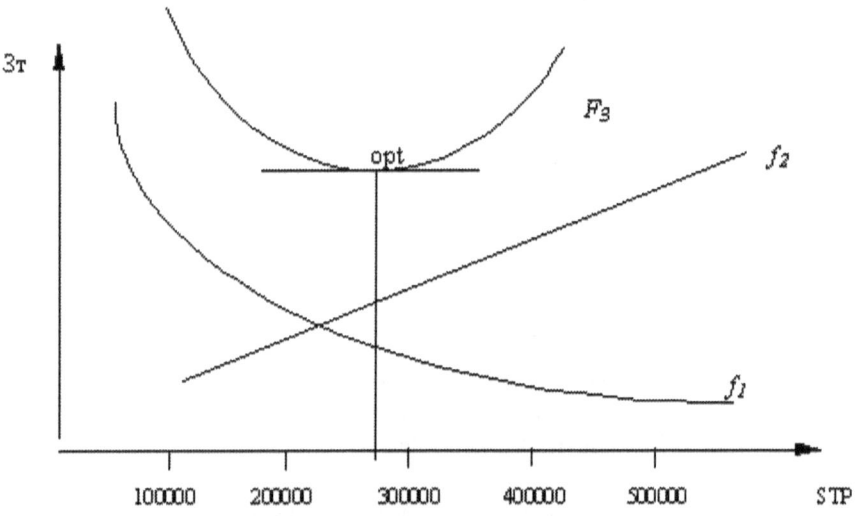

where

A_{STP} assimilated resource of population's spare time; Зт expenses connected with assimilation of STP

f_1 the function of the cost of the current expenses for museum maintenance;

f_2 the function of the expenses related to restoration of works of art;

f_3 is a summary function (f1 + f2);

$$f_3 = (f1 + f2) = 0.$$

Knowing the functions f_1 and f2 makes it easy to determine the values of summary function f3. The first derivative f3 equated with 0, allows us to determine optimum size of the current expenses and restoration charges.

Now let us consider the second component of the formula—V. This V is the size of the museum workers salary. Its value depends on the number of the museum staff and its qualitative composition, as well as on the volume of services offered to the population.

Until present salaries of museum workers are one of the lowest in the national economy. The main reason for this is the fact that the volume of museum services has not been calculated up till now due to an absence of instruments and methods of calculation.

The third component of the formula is M, which is formed as a result of deduction of the expenses spent on commodity production from the cost of commodity output within the frames of material production. It is difficult for a museum to carry out such an arithmetic operation due to the reasons stated above.

The analysis of economic indices of Art museum activities shows that a discrepancy between (C+V) and P is 5.3 times. Thus, for example, annual expenses of this museum (C+V) amounted to 234.6 thousand dollars, and ticket sales gave only 44 thousand dollars.

It should be noted that museum maintenance expenses grow annually because of rising prices of construction and restoration materials while ticket prices remain unchanged for some decades. From my point of view this situation should be revised.

LIBRARY ESTABLISHMENTS

The capital assets of the libraries consist of two parts:
1. A building, system of communications.
2. Material and intellectual values (books, magazines, newspapers, etc.)

During the process of library operation wearing out of the first and second parts of the capital funds proceeds at different «rates». There is a direct analogy with museums:

all depreciation charges should be regarded as a part of the value of library services; depreciation charges for books should not be fixed because the worse the library storage conditions are, the higher the amount of depreciation should be. Therefore, the expenses of creating library services should be higher. The amount of depreciation charges on active part of libraries should be directly matched with the amount of means required for their restoration.

It is known that the salaries of library and museum workers still remain the lowest in the national economy. The basic reason for this lies in the fact that the volume of services produced by this sub-branch have not been calculated yet from a social and economic point of view due to the absence of the required methods.

The third component of the formula is M, which is formed by the deduction of the expenses spent on commodity production from the cost of commodity output within the frames of material production. It is difficult for a library to carry out such an arithmetic operation due to the fact discussed above.

Analysis of economic indices of the universal scientific library activities «enlightenment and entertainment» that the principles contained in the formula are not sustained. Thus, should we sum up only C and V, then it appears that we are operating with economic indices, on one hand, and social indices like «visit», on the other. These two heterogeneous indices cannot be identical and moreover, there is a contradiction between them. Both the right and left part of the formula should be led to one scale to settle the inconsistency. To put it into effect we should first convert «visits» into cost units of measurement.

«TV BROADCASTING» AND «RADIO BROADCASTING»

Problems of value estimation of «enlightenment and entertainment services» under review include for «Television» and «Radio Broadcasting». Until now the volume of services rendered by these branches to the population has been measured by the length of transmission (20-24 hours a day). The drawbacks of this index are in the following: for example, annual expenses for «enlightenment and entertainment services» produced by «Television» are estimated at 1 billion US dollars. This amount of means is equated with the length of transmission, i.e.:

$$1 \text{ billion US dollars} = 8760 \text{ hours (24 hours x 365 days)}$$

These values are not identical. We can only determine a cost price for one hour of operation of «Television» («Radio Broadcast») out of that equation:

$$\frac{1 \text{ billion USD}}{8760 \text{ hours}} = 114155 \text{USD}$$

There is only one way out of this situation: to refuse considering rough analogies with calculations that can be applied to material production while financially estimating results of «enlightenment and entertainment» enterprise activity, and to look into this problem from another angle.

B. NEW ECONOMIC STRUCTURE OF THE «ENLIGHTENMENT AND ENTERTAINMENT SERVICE»

Nowadays Gross National Product (GNP), Gross Domestic Product (GDP), Net Domestic Product (NDP), Net Income (NI) and other economic indicators are calculated with the help of an expense and income method for the branches of the material sphere.

However, it is regretful to admit that the analogous and similar to them indicators are not developed for the intellectual sphere. It would be strange to limit economic thought to material production and not cross the border between those peculiar productions. Thus, for instance, there are nearly 1 billion TV sets in the world. Seventy per cent of TV time is taken by American TV programs and films, which assimilate from 4 to 5 billion hours of the planet's population spare time every day. And the same comes to 1.5-2.0 trillion hours per annum. This circumstance is not considered while estimating the USA's Gross National Product. The indicator is underestimated by 1-2 trillion US dollars during <u>preliminary calculations</u>.

Nowadays the statistics of the intellectual sphere uses very simple indicators: man-visit or man-place. The same goes for enlightenment, art, film distribution and other branches. They inadequately reflect the economic results of the intellectual sphere. Thus, this takes the quality of the administrative decisions in the intellectual sector of national economics to zero.

As for my research, I assert that, if there are distinguishing features between the material and intellectual spheres of production (and they really exist), this is the reason there are futures of material production and there are other methods of calculating indication of intellectual production. This is obvious. Nobody forces us to carry out rough analogies in the methods of calculation, apart from our own subjective factor.

There must be a «spirited», new, «unconventional» calculation of GDP, GNP and NI for the intellectual sphere of production.

In resource extraction branches of material production where the main objective of activity is natural resources extraction (oil, gas, coal and etc.), the value of the resource is included parallel with C, V and R. In other words, the formula will be as follows:

$$C + V + R \text{ resource} = P$$

The analogous logic should be used for the «enlightenment and entertainment branches» as they assimilate (the most valuable resource) the resource of spare time of the population.[38]

If economic theory of the «enlightenment and entertainment branches» drops out of an «exceptional logic» zone and the general economic principles are widely used in it, then the assimilated resource of spare time of the population (STP) should be financially estimated and included into a newly created product.

There are more than enough reasons to include an assimilated resource of spare time into the «enlightenment and entertainment services»:

first, «enlightenment and entertainment service» production is impossible without assimilated resource of the STP, otherwise, a «enlightenment and entertainment service» could not be realized;

second, «enlightenment and entertainment service» consumption takes place during the process of its creation;

third, initial and final phase of «enlightenment and entertainment service» production coincides with the starting and ending phase of consumption;

Inclusion of this new component (in value units of measurement) will modify the structure of a suggested formula. It will be as follows:

$$C + Vi + A_{STP}j + mk = P$$

where:

C—is the cost of past labor related to assimilated resource of the STP;

---

38 As the economic categories «means of production», «instruments of labor», «subjects of labor» are not developed, a logic error has been made when applied to «enlightenment and entertainment branches». Its essence is in the fact that enlightenment and entertainment enterprises assimilate a resource of spare time of the population that is not included into enlightenment and entertainment service value.

Vi—is an essential product, i.e. salary fund of «enlightenment and entertainment» enterprise workers who assimilate resource of the STP;
$A_{STP}j$—is an assimilated resource of STP;
mk—is a surplus product, i.e. profits resulted out of assimilating a resource of the STP (advertising).
i, j, k–imaginary numbers;
P—is «enlightenment and entertainment service» (product of labor of a «enlightenment and entertainment» enterprise).

If in formula $(C + Vi + A_{STP}j + mk = P)$ ASTP is missing, then what resource is assimilated by the past (C) and direct (V + m) labor?
«Enlightenment and entertainment» enterprises do not assimilate any other resource but the population's spare time. It is the only resource that is assimilated by the «enlightenment and entertainment branches».
Based on the above, we can conclude that the exclusion of A_{STP} from the value estimation of «enlightenment and entertainment services» is a big theoretical mistake that understates both the intellectual and general level of welfare of the population.
This theoretical mistake should be corrected.

ECONOMIC EVALUATION OF THE «ENLIGHTENMENT AND ENTERTAINMENT SERVICE»

«Time is money» is a well-known expression. These two categories are interconnected: there is time but no money, there is money but no time. In reality this expression accumulates many problems, which have not been solved in economic theory yet.
When we say «time is money», it is not clarified what part of the time budget of the population is implicated by this. If we speak of working time, the pattern «working time is money» does not raise any negative emotions. It is another thing if we consider the pattern «non-working time is money». There are expenses connected with self-service, cooking, care of children and so on within the frameworks of this temporal bloc. In other words, non-working time is spent on ourselves, on the organization of our everyday life or our families. How can we possibly estimate one hour of «non-working time of a worker» and one hour of «non-working time of a professor»?
If we examine the third bloc of the time budget of the population, namely «spare time of the population», then it will appear that there are also many problems in the pattern «spare time of the population is money». «Spare

time is the wealth of the society» as some of the economists of the past have noted. But it never went any further than popular expressions.

So what part of the spare time of the population is regarded as wealth? This question cannot be answered at once.

I suggest considering such part of the spare time of the population as wealth that has been assimilated by establishments and enterprises of intellectual sphere.

Thus, establishment of «Enlightenment» and «Education» branches assimilate the spare time of the population with the purpose of training required for participation of people in a socially organized process.

The other part of the resource of spare time of the population is assimilated by «enlightenment and entertainment branches» and includes sports entertaining enterprises, branches of «Culture», «Art», «Church», «Television» and «Radio Broadcasting».[39]

ECONOMIC EVALUATION OF THE «MUSEUM SERVICE»

If we use the obtained data in our calculations, then value estimation of assimilated resource of STP by the Art museum can be calculated by the following formula:

$$P = 0,40 \text{ dollar x T M} + K \text{ x V F}$$

where,

P—is a price;

TM—is the resource of spare time of visitors assimilated by the Art museum during a year

0,40—dollar is the cost of one man-hour;

K—is the ticket price in «foreign currency» dollars;

VF—is the number of foreign visitors of the museum

If we apply the given data to this formula, then we are able to estimate that the value of assimilated resource of spare time of museum visiting citizens is 77,000 dollars.

We cannot accept this formula because flow of visitors is not homogeneous at all: part of this flow of visitors can make up to 70 dollars a month but the other part can make up more in a month. Thus, if we refer to the structure of visitors flow of the Art museum sorted out by computer in terms of

---

39 It was defined that cost of one man-hour of spare time is 40 cents.

wage, then we would see that persons of 70 dollars wage make 34,8 per cent but the amount of monthly wage of the rest of the visitors (65,2 per cent) exceeds 70 dollars. Due to this fact I do not think it is appropriate to transfer a cost of one man-hour of spare time (0.4 dollars) of those having wages of 70 dollars on to the persons who make more than that.

In other words, we suggest using values of labor payment as per hour for each of the groups in the calculations of annual services value. Besides this, we need to know the absolute sizes of the assimilated resource of STP for every group of visitors in the context of wages to calculate its cost.

The calculations of the cost of the resource of population spare time assimilated by Art museum are given below:

STRUCTURE OF VISITORS OF THE ART MUSEUM

Index Name	Wages of visitors (in dollars)						
	Up to 70	71-80	81-90	91-100	101-120	121-140	141-160
Labor pay for an hour (in dollars)	0.40	0.43	0.48	0.54	0.62	0.74	0.85
Specific gravity of visitors in %	34.80	2.40	1.10	2.70	6.30	5.80	9.40

Index Name	Wages of visitors (in dollars)						
	161-180	181-200	201-220	221-250	251-300	301-400	more than 400
Labor pay for an hour (in dollars)	0.96	1.07	1.18	1.37	1.56	2.00	2.26
Specific gravity of visitors in %	7.20	9.40	2.90	4.90	5.20	3.00	2.00

%		dollars, cents		in thousand man-hours		Dollars
1.	34.8	x	40	x 194.2	=	27 032
2.	2.4	x	43	x 194.2	=	2 004
3.	1.1	x	48	x 194.2	=	1 153
4.	2.7	x	54	x 194.2	=	2 831
5.	6.3	x	62	x 194.2	=	9 054
6.	5.8	x	74	x 194.2	=	8 335
7.	9.4	x	85	x 194.2	=	15 516
8.	7.2	x	96	x 194.2	=	13 423
9.	9.4	x	1dollar 07 cents.	x 194.2	=	19 532

We have determined that the value of a stationary assimilated resource of STP by the Art museum staff makes 154,700 dollars.

18 700 foreign guests visited the museum. Total amount of receipts came to 267,000 dollars. So, summing up the value of assimilated resource of STP, the annual total is as follows:

$$154{,}746 \text{ dollars} + 267{,}000 \text{ dollars} = 421{,}746 \text{ dollars}$$

If this amount is added with the annual museum expenses (C + V = 234,700 USD), the value of museum services would be as follows per annum:

$$C + V + m + A_{STP} = 234{,}700 + 421{,}746 = 656{,}446 \text{ dollars}$$

It is not the final result of economic activities of the Art museum. We have not taken in consideration the highly efficient traveling form of museum services side by side with stationary services. This is confirmed when analyzing the operation of the museum during the exhibition of Glazunov's paintings. During several weeks of this exhibition, the number of visitors exceeded 200,000.

We can see from the above quoted figures that the growth of the traveling form of services opens wide opportunities to increase the social and economic activities of museums. Summing the transitional result of the economic activities of the Art museum, one can ascertain with great confidence that museum services could be very profitable if everything is organized properly.

When I carried out my studies in the Art museum it seemed to me that none of the museum employees except for their director and the head curator were allowed to the so called custody storage premises. I believe that in this museum as well as in many others there is a great part of displaced cultural values. If this is true, then it is necessary to inspect these values urgently.

For the last 50 years a great number of copies could have been made to change the originals. It is also a very profitable source of income.

Over 1,000 of the art masterpieces from the Hermitage are now in «temporary usage». For example, three tapestries decorate a welcome hall of the Saint Petersberg administration. Two candelabrums light up the days of the Union of Artists. It is recently that they came to their senses and started to check up. It turned out that one candelabrum was really the one of the 12 golden candles casted at the bronze-casting factory of French master Tomir in 1810. The second one is also of the 12 candles but made by an unknown master from an unknown alloy. And where is Mr. Tomir's second one. Nobody knows... Anything may happen to things when they are in temporary usage. A snuff box was returned with a cracked side. A bronze chandelier was returned with cracks and scratches. Anyway, the Russians should be thankful that at least they were returned.

The inspectors of the Chamber of Accounts have looked through the storerooms of the State Hermitage. They have just taken 50 pieces of art at random. They have asked to «enlightenment and entertainment» them. Forty-seven pieces were not available to be shown. A «Mercury» bronze statuette, a marble bosom of Venus, the engravings of «Madonna with an infant» and «Madonna in an armchair», some water color paintings were lost. And then we can go just for the list: three subjects from the Department of the Antique World and 20 pieces from the Department of East.

It is the custodians who are responsible for the masterpieces in any museum. They make sure the exhibits are taken for restoration regularly, and they protect them from any damages accruing during the exhibitions. Over 221,000 exhibits of the Hermitage are attributed to the custodians who have left the museum long ago. The majority of these custodians have already died.

You can see some long rolls with «1947» labels in the same storerooms. Do you really know what this is? They are displaced values. Hundreds of thousands of paintings and many other things were taken out of Europe after the Second World War. Nobody has returned any of them since that period. And nobody has seen them once since that period.

The Hermitage has held nearly one hundred international exhibitions in the past two years. Millions of people from Austria, Holland, France, Japan, United Kingdom and United States have paid money just to see a unique property belonging to Russia. They paid to see the things that only Russia has. And the problem is that Russia itself has practically received nothing from all the exhibitions.

It was only 18 exhibitions out of nearly one hundred that envisaged payment for Russia for giving the paintings. And it is very few that have paid for it.

We Russians, have shown a property of nearly two billion US dollars to the world, and it was just a pleasure for us to show ourselves!

The inspectors of the Chamber of Accounts can hardly believe that. They are especially suspicious because the exhibitions were continuously prolonged. The fact is that if the exhibitions are extended the interest towards them (including a commercial interest) does exist. For example, an exhibition of «200 years of Art with the Shah» was opened in New York, October 24, 1998. The exhibition was to return to Saint Petersburg on January 24, 1999. The period was extended until February 5. It was prolonged for over, not just three month.

The Chamber of Accounts has no right to blame anybody. The only thing it can do is to calculate the losses to the State. The pictures of Candinsky have decorated a museum at the Hague (Netherlands) for three months, yet they were in the position to bring 160,000 US dollars to Russia.

As for the calculations of the Chamber of Accounts, it was possible to get $ 2.4 million provided all the exhibitions stipulate some compensation to Russia for providing the paintings. It was possible to earn at least one million US dollars in the cases when the foreign partners had paid as per the agreements where such the compensation was not stipulated.

And that is not all. Some of the pieces have returned home with damages. An inlaid table of «Flora of Lotaringie» (its cost is one million US Dollar) has returned with some swellings, as the table did not stand up to the temperature overfalls. The inspectors of the Hermitage said that «it was nothing serious and it would dry in the Hermitage». The damage was estimated 12,500 US dollars. Some maniac scratched the painting of Matice with a pen in Rome. The damage was 304,000 US dollars.

In principal, all the damages are covered by insurance. The foreign partners took out the insurance then. But considering the fact that the documents were not made property and damages were found out when the subjects had already returned back to the Hermitage, nothing was paid for the damages. It was necessary to restore them at our own expense.

The Hermitage started with 225 purchased by Ekaterina the Second. Now the collection has 2,893,292 museum subjects. Maybe this is the reason why there is nothing to feel sorry for?[40]

ECONOMIC EVALUATION OF THE «LIBRARY SERVICE»

The Library assimilated 556,400 man-hour of STP at a stationary form during the investigated year. If this result of activities is multiplied by 40 cents, then the cost of assimilated resource STP comes to:

$$A_{STP} = 556,400 \text{ man-hour x } 40 \text{ cents} = 222,600 \text{ dollars}$$

Should we turn our attention to the data of structure of visitors flow of the universal scientific library sorted out by computer in terms of wages, then we will see that the percentage of visitors whose wage is up to 70 dollars makes 44.9 per cent. The rest 55.1 per cent make up the visitors with the monthly wages exceeding 70 dollars.

A calculation of the value of the assimilated resource STP accounting for a structure of visitors is given below:

STRUCTURE OF LIBRARY VISITORS

Index name	Visitor wages (in dollars)						
	up to 70	71-80	81-90	91-100	101-120	121-140	141-160
Labor paid for an hour (in dollars)	0.40	0.43	0.48	0.54	0.62	0.74	0.85
Specific gravity of visitors (in %)	44.9	5.6	21.1	2.7	6.3	5.8	9.4

Index name	Wages of visitors (in dollars)						
	161-180	181-200	201-220	221-250	251-300	301-400	More than 400
Labor paid for an hour (in dollars)	0.96	1.07	1.18	1.37	1.56	2.0	2.26

---

40 Veronica Sivkova «Art for export»

Specific gravity of visitors (in %)	7.2	9.4	2.9	4.9	5.2	3.0	2.0

%		cents		thousand man-hour		dollars
44.9	x	40	x	556.4	=	99 929
5.6	x	43	x	556.4	=	13 398
2.1	x	48	x	556.4	=	5 608
4.1	x	54	x	556.4	=	12 319
8.1	x	62	x	556.4	=	27 943
6.7	x	74	x	556.4	=	27 586
5.8	x	85	x	556.4	=	27 430
5.6	x	96	x	556.4	=	29 912
8.9	x	107	x	556.4	=	52 986
2.4	x	118	x	556.4	=	15 757
2.4	x	137	x	556.4	=	18 294
2.4	x	200	x	556.4	=	7 790
0.3	x	220	x	556.4	=	3 672

TOTAL : 342 623

Value estimation of the assimilated resource of STP with an estimate of a subscription form comes to about 250,000 dollars. The total economic estimation of the volume of spare time assimilated by the library comes to 592,600 dollars.

BREAD PLUS SHOW

It was in ancient Rome that people demanded bread, «enlightenment and entertainment» in quantities adequate for their requirements. If the number of the offered shows decreased, then dissatisfaction of the population could result in replacement of the emperor. A similar situation also seems possible in our days. If for example, TV would be suspended. People are accustomed to «enlightenment and entertainment»—audiovisual services that we cannot live without these days. Shows are the second component of our everyday life, and they find its reflection in the Gross Domestic Product (GDP).

Bread and shows are two essential components of the GDP. Should the leaders of the country forget about one of these two components, then the economy starts "to skid". Now there are no concrete recommendations in economic theory to establish a measure of combination of material and intellectual values. Until now the Gross Domestic Product (GDP) has been calculated based on material activity results. It was mainly grounded on mechanical rather than a political economic basis of A. Smith's and K. Marx's concepts. Its essence is that social production is just a production of material values. I proceed from the assumption that GDP should be formed of material and nonmaterial values and services. Such a broadened point of view reflects social production more accurately and consists of several autonomous spheres—material, intellectual, public health care, military and management. Each one of them correspondingly makes its own part of GDP.

If we consider for example, problems of development of material and intellectual spheres, then naturally we will face the following problem:

What is the ratio between material values and intellectual services in GDP?

POSSIBLE GDP STRUCTURES

Development variant	Material wealth	Intellectual services
A	100%	0%
B	80%	20%
C	60%	40%
D	50%	50%
E	40%	60%
F	20%	80%
G	0%	100%

In case the structure of social production is developed according to variant A, then all the resources will be directed towards the production of material values and their maximum would be achieved. If social production is developed according to variant G, then all resources of the society are directed towards production of intellectual services and their maximum would be achieved.

Even in ancient Rome they sought for optimum proportion between «bread» and «shows». The problem is actual today, too.

In connection with this we can suggest the following possible structure of the activity results based on the two components: «bread» and «shows» (accounting for an assimilated resource STP).

POSSIBLE STRUCTURE OF RESULTS OF ONE COUNTRY

Year	Bread		Shows (Assimilated resource STP)	
	Production volume	%	Production volume	%
1985	50 million tons	100	20 billion hours	100
1988	45 million tons	90	21 billion hours	105
1992	40 million tons	80	22 billion hours	110
1993	35 million tons	70	23 billion hours	115
1995	30 million tons	60	24 billion hours	120
1997	50 million tons	100	24 billion hours	120

If we proceed with the assumption that one ton of wheat is evaluated at 100 US dollars and one hour of STP at 0,40 US dollar, then we can calculate possible GDP in value units of measurement.

VALUE ESTIMATION OF ASSUMED GDP OF ONE COUNTRY
BY TWO COMPONENTS: «BREAD—SHOWS»

Years	Bread			Shows			GDP	
	Production volume	% by 1985 year	Value estimation of assimilated STP resource	Enlightenment and entertainment branches costs to assimilated STP resource	% by 1985 year	in billion US $	% by 1985 year
1985	50 million tons x 100 = $5 billion US	100	20 billion hours x 0,4 = $8 billion US	100 million US dollars	100	13.10	100.0
1988	45 million tons x 100 = $4,5 billion US	90	21 billion hours x 0,4 = $8,4 billion US	100 million US dollars	105	13.00	99.2
1992	40 million tons x 100 = $4,0 billion US	80	22 billion hours x 0,4 = $8,8 billion US	100 million US dollars	110	12.90	98.5
1993	35 million tons x 100 = $3,5 billion US	70	23 billion hours x 0,40 = $9,2 billion US	100 million US dollars	115	12.80	97.7
1995	30 million tons x 100 = $3 billion US	60	24 billion hours x 0,40 = $9,6 billion US	100 million US dollars	120	12.70	96.9

The above calculations make it possible:

First: to carry out calculations of an immaterial part of the gross domestic product (GDP) created in the frames of the «enlightenment and entertainment branches».

Second: to bridge the substantial gap in the GDP calculations.

ECONOMIC ELAVUATION OF THE US «ENLIGHTENMENT AND ENTERTAINMENT SERVICE»

If, for instance, a «enlightenment and entertainment» enterprise assimilates 170 billion hours of STP and expenses on equipment (C) cost 50 billion dollars, the wage fund (V) 20 billion dollars and profits (m) 50 million dollars, then A_{STP} is left unknown, i.e. the value of the assimilated resource of the population's spare time. The newly created volume of «enlightenment and entertainment services» P («enlightenment and entertainment» product) cannot be calculated without it.

If we proceed from the fact that the minimum wage in the USA, in 1988, was US $ 3.35 an hour then,

$$170 \text{ billion hours x US } \$ 3.35 = \text{US } \$ 569.5 \text{ billion.}$$

The value of a newly created «enlightenment and entertainment» product can be calculated as follows:

$$C + V + m + A_{STP} = P$$

that is

US $ 50 billion + US $ 20 billion + US $ 50 million + US $ 569.5 billion = US $689.5 billion

CHAPTER 11

DEVELOPMENT AND ALLOCATION OF PRODUCTIVE FORCES IN THE «ENLIGHTENMENT AND ENTERTAINMENT BRANCHES»

An analysis of the economic literature reveals that the problems of expanded reproduction of the material sphere are more or less covered. However, there is no theory of expanded reproduction in the «enlightenment and entertainment branches».

The «enlightenment and entertainment branches» faces problems in development possibilities—building or reconstructing its enterprises, expanded production of intellectual services in branch-wise and region-wise aspects of consideration. However, until now it was difficult to maintain an economically rational policy of developing «enlightenment and entertainment» enterprises due to subjective reasons.

A consideration of the problems of «enlightenment and entertainment branches» development is conditioned, firstly, by an increase in the population's spare time resource, and, secondly, by the need to distribute labor, material and financial resources between regions and cities economically and rationally. It is natural that every region should develop those types and forms of «enlightenment and entertainment» activities, which are most favorable from an ethnographic point of view. This fact must be considered when specializing «enlightenment and entertainment» enterprises and institutions.

The heart of the problems in «enlightenment and entertainment service» expanded reproduction lie in defining strategic directions for the «enlightenment and entertainment branches» in order to reach a high level of intellectual provision with minimum labor expenses.

A. A SINGLE-PRODUCT MODEL OF THE DEVELOPMENT OF THE «ENLIGHTENMENT AND ENTERTAINMENT BRANCHES»

I propose to consider the problems of «enlightenment and entertainment branches» development and «enlightenment and entertainment» enterprise allocation by using <u>a narrow-single-product and a broad-multi-product interpretation.</u>

The difference in these two interpretations is the specialization of the one-type enterprises of the «enlightenment and entertainment branches», which produce the «enlightenment and entertainment services», <u>in the first case.</u> They use similar technologies for assimilating the spare time resource of a population. A multi-factor model is considered <u>in the second case.</u>

Economic and mathematical methods can help to solve the above problems. A particular feature of using these methods is that the assimilated spare time resource of a population and other estimated economic indicators.

A graphic interpretation of the development and placement of «enlightenment and entertainment branches» productive forces may be presented as follows. There is homogenous transport surface, on which «enlightenment and entertainment» enterprises A and B are located in a certain pattern. They assimilate the population's spare time resource by the same technology as expenditures C_A and C_B respectively. Transport costs per 1 km will be designated as S_r. It is obvious that with concrete cost values it is possible to find geometrical points, which compensate the difference in the cost of developing the population's spare time resource. This constant is a line that divides the influence of enterprise sphere A and B, and at the same time determines a length within which they are under equal production conditions. This has a graphic interpretation, as follows (Dr. 7.1) and meets the following requirement:

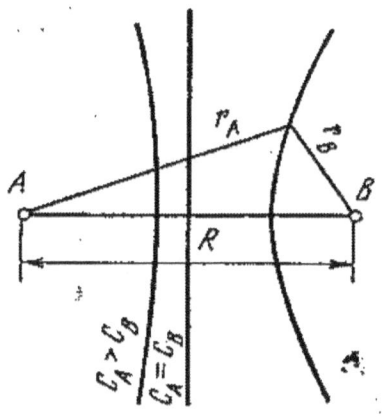

(Dr. 7.1)

$$C_A + S \cdot r_A = C_A + S \cdot r_B.$$

For the points lying on the optimum border, the difference in distance from each of them to enterprises A and B is a constant value, determined as follows:

$$r_A - r_B = \frac{C_A - C_B}{S}$$

From the above drawing it can be seen that costs of «enlightenment and entertainment service» production, located to the right of the optimum line are higher for B than for A at B-institution is higher then at A. At the same time, in the sphere of influence, of enterprise A to the left of this constant costs are higher than for enterprise B. The task can be graphically interpreted for a larger number of ««enlightenment and entertainment branches».

If we make the specific expenses of labor decrease in proportion to the increasing volume of the assimilated STP resource and the transport expenses in direct proportional dependence on the territorial remoteness of the objects being serviced, a summary production function can be written as follows:

$$f(A\ (t)) + f(r\ (t)) + f(r_s\ (t)) = f_s.$$

where

$f(A\ (t))$ - function of the expenses for stationary assimilation of the population's spare time resource,

$f(r\ (t))$ - function of transport expenses,

$f(r_s\ (t)]$ - function of expenses connected with production of these services a mobile form of servicing.

This target appears graphically as follows:

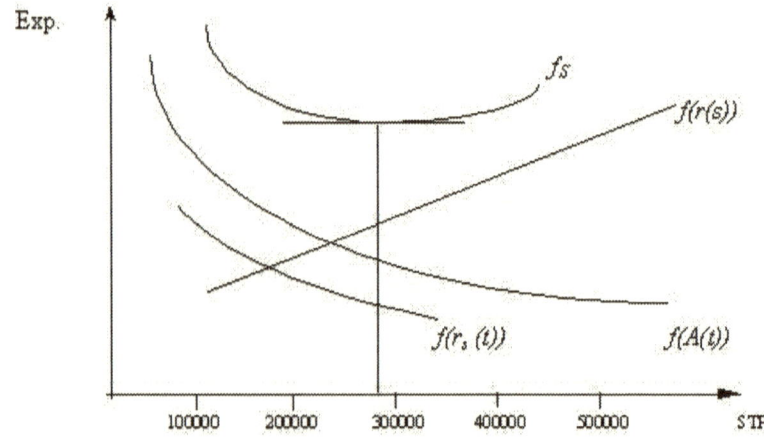

Proceeding with the above conditions, it is necessary to set up an optimum variant for assimilating the population's spare time resource «enlightenment and entertainment» enterprise's personnel in stationary and mobile forms of servicing, on the condition of keeping the given expenses to a minimum.

By equating the first derivative of the summary function to zero ($f_s = 0$), we find the critical points that we need.

For instance, the aim of finding the optimum volume of the assimilated spare time resource for a population is achieved as follows for two TV centers:

$$\begin{cases} S_1 = V_1 \cdot N_1 + C_1 \\ S_2 = V_2 \cdot N_2 + C_2 \end{cases} \qquad \begin{matrix} (I) \\ (II) \end{matrix}$$

, where

S$_1$ and S2—expenses of assimilating people's spare time resource by the first and second TV centers;

V$_1$ and V2—conditional variable expenses of assimilating one man-hour of the people's spare time by the first and second TV centers;

N$_1$ and N2—volume of the assimilated resource of the people's spare time by the first and second TV centers;

C$_1$ and C2—conditional-constant expenses of the first and second TV centers respectively.

A graphic solution to the equations (I) and (II) for two TV centers is given below:

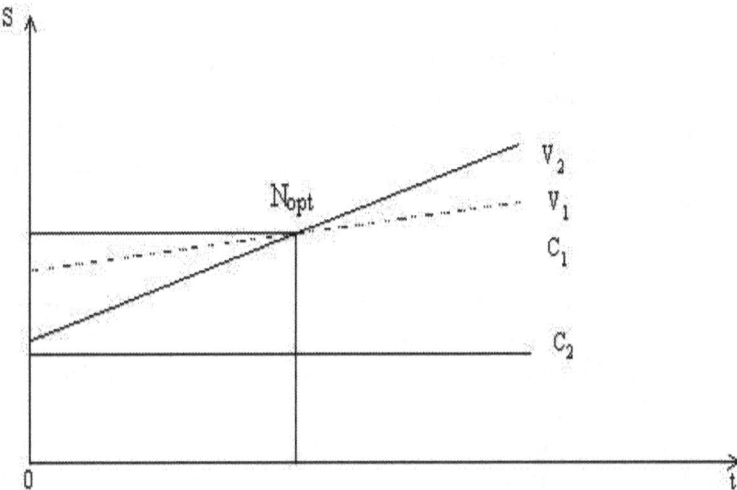

At point N the cost of assimilating one hour of the people's spare time in a region will be the same for both the first and the second TV centers.

N$_{opt}$ is calculated as follows:

$$N_{opt} = \frac{C_1 - C_2}{V_2 - V_1}$$

The above graphic interpretation of «enlightenment and entertainment» enterprise development forms a logical basis for forming economic mathematical models:
- statistical models;
- dynamic models for specializing these enterprises and institutions in the
  context of their material and technical basis, labor resources and accounting for social demographic and ethnographic peculiarities of the assimilated spare time resource of the population.

At present the targets and tasks for development and allocation of the «enlightenment and entertainment branches» productive forces are achieved mostly
by intuition and without wide utilization of economic mathematical methods in administration. The delay in solving this cycle of targets and tasks is
conditioned by:
- first, the absence of the socio-economic characteristics required for meeting the targets of «enlightenment and entertainment branches»;
- second, the absence of socio-economic effectiveness criteria for utilizing
  the resources of the «enlightenment and entertainment branches»;
- third, the absence of any research into the particular features of utilizing
  economic-mathematical methods in the «enlightenment and entertainment branches».

One should note that the main features for applying economic and mathematical methods are as follows:
1.   Formalized record of a system of quantified characteristics;
2.   Formalized record of a system aiming towards its achievement;
3.   Imposing limitations on the means of achieving a system's aim;
4.   Interchangeability of the means included in the process of assimilating
      the population's spare time resource.

A general model of mathematical programming in the «enlightenment and
entertainment branches» would appear as follows:

$$\begin{cases} max\ (min)\ Z = f & (t_1, t_2, \dots t_n) \\ 3_i\ (t_1, t_2, \dots t_n) <= b_i & (i= 1, 2, \dots m) \\ t_j >= 0 & (j = 1, 2, \dots n) \end{cases}$$

where

Z —optimized aim of the «enlightenment and entertainment branches»;

$f(t_1, t_2 \ldots t_n)$ —aim function of the «enlightenment and entertainment branches»

—the population's spare time resource assimilated;

$3_i(t_1, t_2 \ldots t_n)$ —function of collective expenditures of i-means, used to assimilate the population's spare time resource;

b_i —limitations on i-resources used.

The criteria for socio-economic efficiency worked out by the author, allow us to determine which variant of economic strategy of «enlightenment and entertainment» activities' development should be looked at. Special features of these criteria include economic-mathematical models of optimum planning and algorithms of «enlightenment and entertainment branches» development.

The solution of tasks of branch planning and development and the placement of «enlightenment and entertainment branches» productive forces allows us to establish a specialization of «enlightenment and entertainment» enterprises and an optimum structure of services. It would also allow a selection of an optimum variant for building up new enterprises and closing unproductive ones.

The essence of the long-term effectiveness criterion is that it is not the general volume of «enlightenment and entertainment service» production, but its increased portion dV, on the one hand, and the amount of increment of the means causing it, on the other, that forms the target, i.e.

$$\text{The correlation } \frac{dV}{dK} \text{ must tend towards the maximum,}$$

The following scheme is possible based upon a dual structure of labor expenses in «enlightenment and entertainment branches» production:

A SYSTEM OF CRITERIA
OF «LONG-TERM EFFECTIVENESS»

$$1. \text{«Thesis» criterion} = \frac{\text{ncrement } (\Delta) \text{ of assimilated STP resource}}{\text{Additional } (\Delta) \text{ expenses of past labor}}$$

$$2. \text{«Antithesis» criterion} = \frac{\text{Increment } (\Delta) \text{ of assimilated STP resource}}{\text{Additional } (\Delta V) \text{ expenses of direct labor}}$$

$$3. \text{«Synthesis» criterion} = \frac{\text{Increment } (\Delta) \text{ of assimilated STP resource}}{\text{Additional } (\Delta) \text{ expenses of aggregate labor}}$$

The criteria of effectiveness, which the author has worked out, (maximizing the assimilation of the spare time resource of a population and minimizing the expenses of direct and past labor), put a definite emphasis on economic-mathematical methods and models. These particular «dual estimates» allow an expansion of the utilization and geography of these methods.

Utilization of these methods allows for the setting up of an optimum amount and territorial allocation of «enlightenment and entertainment branches» enterprises and specialization the «enlightenment and entertainment» enterprises. It allows for the setting up of an optimum structure for the «enlightenment and entertainment services» and also for choosing an optimum variant for expanding (constructing) new enterprises and closing down unproductive ones.

It is necessary to note that at present the criteria values of resource utilization functionally depend upon the afore mentioned investment policy. Applied to the «enlightenment and entertainment branches», if the construction of «enlightenment and entertainment» enterprises took place in the territories, that the people moved from, the criteria of their effectiveness would continue to decline. But the opposite is true.

B. A MULTI-PRODUCT MODEL OF THE DEVELOPMENT OF THE «ENLIGHTENMENT AND ENTERTAINMENT BRANCHES»

Problems in the current and long-term development of «enlightenment and entertainment branches» productive forces are very closely connected. Thus, current planning is oriented towards, on the one hand, development of the spare time resource and, on the other, rational use of the existing elements of materials and technology, the labor force in the relevant sectors and in fixed territorial limits. Correct decisions made in the development and placement of the above factors depends both on the future and current characteristics of «enlightenment and entertainment» activity efficiency.

Working out optimum decisions in this sphere depends mostly on the time factor and on economic, ethnographic and other special features of the particular region.

In order to solve the above problems it is necessary to formulate an economic-mathematical model of the development and placement of «enlightenment and entertainment branches» productive forces. Any determined value appearing in it is a function of «enlightenment and entertainment service» production for each enterprise in any region. A regional population's spare time may be increased at the expense of the reconstruction, functioning and building of new institutions, by using a mobile form of service as well as by closing down activities and institutions where costs of production are high.

In other words, it is necessary out of the whole variety of possible variants, for a region to select an optimum one, taking into account all the possible limitations on material and financial resources, the labor force and the potential spare time resource.

It is only possible to achieve this task provided each variant of the development network of different «enlightenment and entertainment» production institutions corresponds to an estimation system on the basis of which a prospective or non-prospective variant of development will be determined.

Producing a development and placement model of production productive forces relies on the selection of a variant for the development and functioning of the institutions of this sphere, construction site location and specialization of new institution, as well as on using a mobile form of service with set volumes of assimilating the population's spare time. Also to be taken into account are the nature of the technologies to be used in the future, based on capital investment limitations, on the one hand, and minimizing particular and total expenses, on the other.

Establishing an optimum correlation between the development of MTB and the labor forces in «enlightenment and entertainment branches» productive forces is achieved by comparing given expenditures in each possible variation.

The expenditures presented in such a sphere of production can be written as follows:

$$Exv_i = \sum_{l \in L} \sum_{j \in J} \sum_{i \in I} (C_{ijl} \cdot T_{ijl} + E_H^j \cdot K_{ijl}) \rightarrow \min$$

where

C_{ijl}—prospective expenses of production of i-unit «enlightenment and entertainment services» at institutions in j-branch in l-region;

T_{ijl}—volume of production of i-services at j-institution in l-region;

EJH—corrective coefficient (ratio) of prospective efficiency expenditures directed to extended reproduction of i-«enlightenment and entertainment services» in j-branch of this sphere in l-region.

K_{ijl}—volume of expenditures directed to extended reproduction of i-«enlightenment and entertainment services» in j-branch of this sphere in l-region.

On the basis of this formula of the expenditures in «enlightenment and entertainment branches», the annual economic effect of using a more productive economic version compared to a less productive one, when considering a single product, can be written as follows:

$$Э = \left(C_1 \cdot T_1 + E_н^к \cdot K_1 \right) - \left(C_2 \cdot T_2 + E_н^к \cdot K_2 \right)$$

, where

C_1, C_2—prospective cost of production of j-«enlightenment and entertainment services» under compared variants I and II respectively;

T_1, T_2—volume of «enlightenment and entertainment services» production on I and II variants respectively;

E—corrective (ratio) of production expenses expenditures directed to extend reproduction of «enlightenment and entertainment services» on I and II variants respectively.

The total annual economic effect of using an optimum variant of development and placement of «enlightenment and entertainment branches» productive forces, when considering multiple products, can be written as follows:

$$\Theta_{o\delta\,\upsilon} = \sum_{l=1}\sum_{j=1}\sum_{i=1}\left(C^{j}_{ijl}\cdot T_1 + E^{\kappa\,j.}_{\mu}K^{l}_{ijl}\right) - \left(C^{l}_{ijl}\cdot T_2 + E^{\kappa\,j.}_{\mu}K^{l}_{2jl}\right)$$

The corrective term for payment of capital investments into the development of «enlightenment and entertainment branches» is determined as follows:

$$T^{\mathcal{A}}_{\mu} = \frac{1}{E^{\mathcal{A}}_{\mu}}$$

where

T—a term of repayment in the «enlightenment and entertainment branches»;

E—corrective ratio (coefficient) of efficient investments in the «enlightenment and entertainment branches».

CONVENTIONAL SIGNS

i —index of institutions producing «enlightenment and entertainment services»;

I_1 —number of enterprises functioning in the «enlightenment and entertainment branches»;

I_2 —number of enterprises that are being built over a given period;

l —«enlightenment and entertainment service» nomenclature;

LI_1 —«enlightenment and entertainment service»—nomenclature number of institutions functioning;

LI_2 —«enlightenment and entertainment service»—nomenclature number of institutions newly built;

r —index of a variant of «enlightenment and entertainment branches» productive forces development and placement;

R_1 —number of variants of functioning institutions' development;

R_2 —number of variants of «enlightenment and entertainment branches» under reconstruction and in the process of construction in populated areas where there already are such enterprises;

$T^{r}il$ —volume of assimilated resource of the population's spare time by i-institution when using a stationary form of service on l-technology on r-variant of development;

$C^{r}il$ —expenses connected to the assimilation of 1 hour of the population's spare time at i-enterprise that is being constructed on l-technology on r-variant of development;

$K^{r}il$ —share capital expenditure needed for realization of r-variant of development of i-institution on l-technology;

j —index of stationary institutions producing «enlightenment and entertainment service» in a hypothetical plan;

TJ —number of j-stationary institutions, which are in under construction, producing «enlightenment and entertainment service» in, populated areas, where there are no such institutions;

R_3 —number of variants of introduction of new j-«enlightenment and entertainment branches»;

R_4 —number of variants of a mobile form of servicing;

LI_3 —nomenclature number of «enlightenment and entertainment service» enterprises, which are under construction in the given branch in populated areas where there are no such enterprises;

$T^{r}jl$ —potential resource of the population's spare time in j-populated area hypothetically assimilated on l-technology;

$C^{r}jl$ —hypotethical expenses connected to the assimilation of 1 hour of the population's spare time at j-institution on l-technology at r-variant of development and placement;

$K^{r}jl$ —share capital investments needed for implementing r-variant of development of j-institutions producing hypothetically l-nomenclature of «enlightenment and entertainment service»;

E —corrective coefficient of capital investment efficiency in the «enlightenment and entertainment branches»;

$T^{r}ijl$ —expenses connected with moving a portion of material resources and labor forces of i-«enlightenment and entertainment» enterprises into j-populated areas for assimilating of the population's spare time resource there;

$C^{r}ijl$ —share capital investments in vehicles needed for a mobile form of service for the population in j-populated area;

$K^{r}ijl$ —hypothetical volume of assimilation of the population's spare time resource in j-populated area on l-technology;

T_1 —number of populated areas in which it's possible to implement a mobile form of service;

LI_4 —nomenclature number of «enlightenment and entertainment service» applied when using a mobile form of service;

$P_{\text{д}}$ —coefficient of discounting.

The target function appears as follows:

$$F(t) = \sum_{l \in LI_1} \sum_{i \in I_2, r \in R_1} C_{il}^r t_{il}^r Z_{il}^r +$$

$$+ \sum_{l \in LI} \sum_{i \in I_2, \varpi R_2} (C_{il}^r + E_H^{\text{Д}} K_{il}^r) \cdot t_{il}^r Z_{il}^r \cdot P_{\text{д}} +$$

$$+ \sum_{l \in LI_3} \sum_{j \in J_2, \varpi R_3} (C_{jl}^r + E_H^{\text{Д}} K_{jl}^r) \cdot t_{jl}^r Z_{ijl}^r \cdot P_{\text{д}} +$$

$$+ \sum_{l \in LI_4} \sum_{j \in J_2, r \in R_4} (C_{ijl}^r + E_H^{\text{Д}} K_{ijl}^r) \cdot t_{jl}^r Z_{ijl}^r \cdot P_{\text{д}} \rightarrow \textbf{min}$$

$$t_{il} \ i \ 0, t_{jl} > 0$$

UNDER THE FOLLOWING LIMITATIONS:

1. The volume of the population's assimilated spare time resource at r-variant of development cannot be higher than its potential possible value within the framework of i-institution possible when using l-technology:

$$\sum_{l \in LI} \sum_{r \in R_1} t_{il}^r \cdot Z_{il}^r \leq T_{il}^r; \ (i \in I_1 \cup I_2), (r \in R_1 \cup R_2), (l \in LI_1 \cup LI_2)$$

2. The hypothetical volume of production and consumption of «enlightenment and entertainment services» at j-institution on r-variant of development when using a mobile form of service must not exceed the population's
spare time potential resource, namely:

$$\sum_{l \in LI} \sum_{r \in R_2} t_j^r \cdot Z^r \leq T_j^r; \ (j \in I_1 \cup I_2), \ (r \in R_1 \cup R_2), \ (1 \in LI_1 \cup LI_2)$$

3. Limitations on the volume of capital investments:

a) $K_j^r \leq K$;

b) $K_i^r \leq K$;

c) $K_{ij}^r \leq K$;

d) $K \geq \begin{cases} K_{il} \\ K_{jl} \\ K_{ijl} \end{cases}$.

Each of these items may be considered from the angle of limitations on material resources as well as on labor forces.

4. Parameters for changing the additional variable assuming two values:

$Z_i^r = 1$, $Z_j^r = 1$, if a variant of development is prospective,

$Z_i^r = 0$, $Z_j^r = 0$, if a variant is non-prospective.

C. NETWORK PLANNING AND MANAGEMENT IN THE «ENLIGHTENMENT AND ENTERTAINMENT BRANCHES»

Within the framework of a city or region, «enlightenment and entertainment»
enterprises appear as a complex socio-economic system with external and
internal factors oriented towards the creation of «enlightenment and enter-

tainment services». Both current and long term planning for the system under consideration is a rather complex task, which may be to some extent, in my opinion, by using net methods.

At present time the need to extend the sphere of application of net methods, especially in the «enlightenment and entertainment branches», is growing.

Network planning and management is a combination of both graphical and calculus methods that allow modeling of the production process, taking into account changes to the situation both in and outside production. These methods are the basis for the mechanism of construction, and calculation and optimizing network models. Besides which they serve as a basis for construction of network planning and management systems (PMS).

Application of network methods in the «enlightenment and entertainment branches» is necessary to simplify the preparation of «enlightenment and entertainment» programs for a city or region for rational use of the material, financial and labor resources of these institutions, as well as improving the quality of work.

In my opinion, a network model of «enlightenment and entertainment» enterprise activities in a region must be a complex of work, inter-related and systematized in time and space, directed at achieving high social and economic results. We see this network as an oriented chart reflecting the relations between the various kinds of work involved in the preparation of «enlightenment and entertainment» measures.

Network planning of «enlightenment and entertainment» enterprise activities for a region must be carried out in several interrelated stages:

1. Description of all «enlightenment and entertainment» measures (EEM) and of the work needed for their implementation in a month, week, quarter, half year, year;
2. Determination of time intervals for each kind of SM by executives;
3. Working out a general network graph;
4. Determination of critical course and time reserves of network graphs for «enlightenment and entertainment» activities;
5. Analysis of optimizing network graphs for «enlightenment and entertainment» activities.

PARAMETERS OF A NETWORK GRAPH OF «ENLIGHTENMENT AND ENTERTAINMENT» ENTERPRISE ACTIVITIES

Construction of a network graph is only possible if a list of «enlightenment and entertainment» measures (EEM) has been determined and the terms for their implementation established. This will allow us to break the preparation of each measurement into components and attach certain variables to them.

Determining the duration of this or that phase of preparation of EEM in mandays is carried out by highly competent show-men, specialists, based on experience of implementating similar measures and taking into account factors that can speed up or slow down the preparation processes. An expert estimate of a method to establish the preparation time for the measures may be employed here.

Stages of preparation and implementation are presented in succession, reflecting their interrelation.

One should note that constructing a network graph for activities of «enlightenment and entertainment» enterprises is based on the same principles used for network graphs in the material sphere. The only difference is that here we have stages for the preparation for measurements concerning the organization of the population's spare time.

Time is the main parameter, on the basis of which a network graph is constructed. This covers both the duration of the preparation of this or that stage of measurements and date of implementation. Time is taken as a basis for such parameters of a network graph as «critical course» and «time reserves for implementing enlightenment and entertainment measures».

A critical variable is the longest in terms duration of all the jobs undertaken—from the start to finish of conducting a «enlightenment and entertainment» measurement. It directly depends on the duration of particular stages of work. That is why, in a process of managing «enlightenment and entertainment» activities on a regional scale, it is necessary to concentrate on a «critical course»: to plan the kinds of work promptly, which will directly influence the terms for implementing «enlightenment and entertainment» measures assimilating STP. By the way, a regional network graph may contain several «critical courses».

The other courses of a network graph are not critical. The courses closest in duration to the critical ones are called sub-critical courses. All kinds of work in the preparation of non-critical course measurements have some reserves of time, i. e. terms of preparation and fulfillment can be «flexible» to a certain extent.

A time reserve is another main parameter of a network graph, since calculation of time reserves serves as a basis for making decisions concerning the reduction of a length of a critical course.

The reserves are the length of within which occurrence of an event may be delayed (a stage of work) without breaking the terms for completing the preparation and implementation «enlightenment and entertainment» measures as a whole. The time reserve is determined as follows:

$$P = T_n - T_p;$$

where

T_n—top limit of the duration of work for a particular stage, the exceeding of which will cause a breach in the terms of conducting «enlightenment and entertainment» measurements or cultural events;

T_p—lower limit of implementing a particular stage of preparation.

It is determined by choosing a maximum value of duration from all the courses, leading to conducting a given «enlightenment and entertainment» measurement.

The above can be presented in the following formula:

$$T_{pi} = t \, [\, L_{max} \, (I \div i)],$$

$$T_{ni} = t \, (L_{kp}) - t \, [L_{max} \, (i \div C)],$$

where

I -starting event (beginning of preparation of EEM);

C-concluding event (date of conducting EEM).

The full reserve time of course $R(_{Li})$ is the difference between the length of a critical course $t(L_{kp})$ and the length of any other course $t(L_i)$, written as follows:

$$R(L_i) = t(L_{kp}) - t(L_i),$$

where

R (Li) shows by what duration the total sum may be increased for of all kinds of work belonging to the course L_i, i.e. the maximum permissible increase in the duration of all kinds of work on the L_i—course.

The first reserve of time of the Rnij job is determined by the following formula:

$$R_{nij} = T_{nj} - T_{pi} - t_{ij}$$

A graphical representation of the opportunities for using reserves of time for «enlightenment and entertainment» works appears as follows:

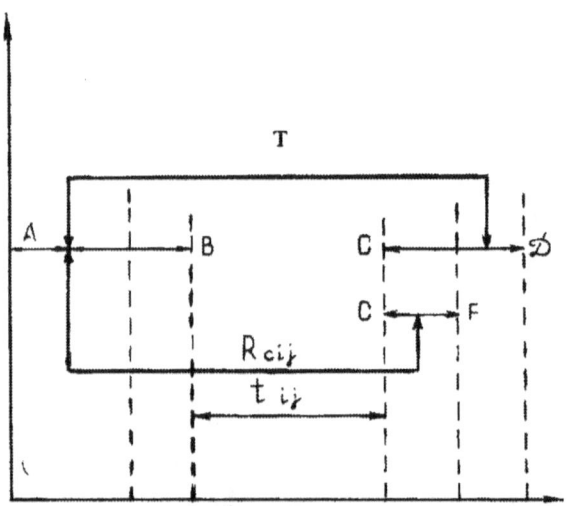

One should note that separate stages of preparation for «enlightenment and entertainment» measurement on the organization of STP, apart from the full reserve of time (Rnij), also have a free time reserve. This means that there is a maximum amount of time by which the duration of these stages may be increased or their beginning held over, provided the stage has begun early on.

Using a free reserve of time showmen can maneuver within its borders (limits) begin an independent job. Without Rcij, room to maneuver disappears.

The full reserve of time is equal to the sum of two lengths.

$$AB\ (R_i = T_{ni} - T_{pi})\ and\ CD\ (R_j = T_{nj} - T_{pi}),$$

While the sum of the length AB and C'F is equal to a value of the free reserve—Rcij.

The classification and grouping of works into full and free time reserves and the establishment of degrees of difficulty of each work group may be achieved by using a tension ratio. This is basically a comparison of the duration of non-coinciding lengths of a course, one of maximum duration going through a given work and the other, a critical course.

In formula form, a tension ratio of the «enlightenment and entertainment» activities can be written as follows:

$$K_{nij} = 1 - \frac{R_{n\,ij}}{t(L_{kp}) - t'(L_{kp})}$$

where

$t'(L_{kp})$—value of the length of a course.

The higher the value of the tension ratio, the more difficult the fulfillment of a job is within set terms. Conversely, the lower its value, the more time reserves there are for finishing a given job.

It should be noted that for each executive drawings may be constructed of his/her loading with graphic representation of the volume of work attached to him/her. This will endow him/her to manipulate the spare time resources thus improving the quality of «enlightenment and entertainment» measurements.

OPTIMIZATION OF A NETWORK GRAPH OF A «CULTURAL» BRANCH INSTITUTION'S ACTIVITIES

Focusing the activities of «enlightenment and entertainment» enterprises in critical directions, within the framework of network planning tasks is, in my opinion, possible at the expense of the redistribution of personnel, materials and technology (decoration, musical instruments, equipment, books, pictures, etc.)

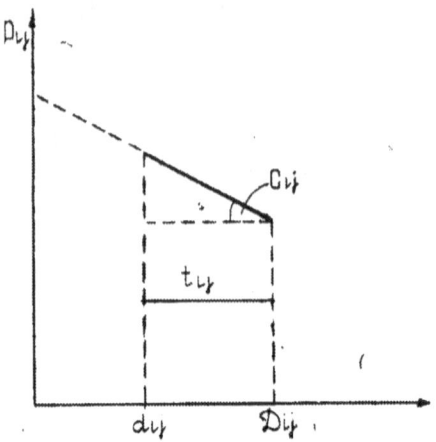

«Time—cost of CEI»

The set aim for us is to find the optimum correlation of the expenditure of
executives' working time and the terms of conducting «enlightenment and
entertainment» measures. In particular, lies the essence of optimizing a
network graph of a «enlightenment and entertainment» enterprise activity
model.

The below algorithms for optimizing network graphs are based on the fact that
the cost of «enlightenment and entertainment» measurement preparation
is directly proportional to the duration of its preparation.

The cost of a separate stage of «enlightenment and entertainment» measurement preparation P_{ij} at duration tij can be written as follows:

$$P_{ij} = K_{ij} - t_{ij} C_{ij},$$

where C_{ij}—proportional growth ratio on a unit of development of the spare
time resource.

If at all the stages, the normal (average) duration of EEM preparation has been
chosen, then a plan of «enlightenment and entertainment» enterprise activities will have a total duration D_n. In this case, if accelerated duration dn
is chosen, then an accelerated plan of EEM preparation will be possible.
However this does not mean that in a given duration (dn), the plan of preparation will assume an optimum value. This can be reduced at the expense
of prolonging non-critical tasks in SM preparation.

Minimizing expenditure on «enlightenment and entertainment» enterprise activities is achieved as below. It is necessary to find a succession of numbers, which would meet the following requirements:

$$d_{ij} \leq t_{ij} \leq D_{ij}$$

$$\sum_{(ij)\in U} t_{ij} \leq t_{\text{н}} \qquad \text{for all } C$$

$$\sum_{(ij)\in U} (K_{ij} - C_{ij}t_{ij}) = \boldsymbol{min}$$

where ij—number of all the courses connecting the beginning and the end of the network;

t_H—time of SM preparation with minimum extra expenditure, taken as the total sum of all additional resources, allocated for separate tasks during the optimizing of all aspects (nomenclature) of «enlightenment and entertainment» measures.

When considering $t_H = 1$ at a variable parameter, the task reduces the chance of solving a task of parametrical linear programming:

$$d_{ij} \leq t_{ij} \leq D_{ij}$$

$$\sum_{(ij)\in U} t_{ij} \leq \lambda \qquad \text{for all } \in$$

$$\sum_{(ij)\in U} C_{ij}t_{ij} = max$$

Optimizing a network graph of «enlightenment and entertainment» enterprises' activities may also be solved as a task (of flow) of convex piece-linear programming:

$$\sum_{(ij)\in U'_i} \varphi_{ij} \begin{cases} 0, i \neq 1, \ i \neq n \\ -\Phi, i = n \\ \Phi, i = 1 \end{cases}$$

$$\lambda\Phi + \sum_{ij\in U} D_{ij} \, max[\, 0, C_{ij} - \varphi_{ij}] - \sum_{ij\in U} d_{ij} \, max[\, 0, \varphi_{ij} - C_{ij}] = min$$

where j_{ij}, Φ—non-negative double variables.

Existing algorithms of optimizing a network graph allow as to determine a complex task (time expenditures) reduction that may be effective and yield a desirable result. Critical tasks are interrelated with uncritical ones, which is why it is very important to determine by what value particular critical tasks may be reduced, i.e. to take into account the position of each critical task in a network graph. The level of reduction in critical work depends on the availability of uncritical tasks that are parallel to critical ones, and the amount of reserve time spent on these tasks. In reducing critical works, which has parallel tasks, one should be guided by the following rules: the permissible level of reduction in the duration of critical tasks is equal to the full time reserve of a parallel uncritical task. In such case, the total duration of «enlightenment and entertainment» measurement preparation may be reduced by precisely the same value.

If together with a critical task, several uncritical ones come out of the same vertex, then a possible value of reduction in the duration of a critical task is determined by the minimum reserve on uncritical tasks. Here I should note that if full reserve is used on at least one task in the parallel uncritical chain, then this chain is deprived of all reserves and takes a critical course. We will consider the variants:

a) Critical tasks does not have parallel tasks. In this case, critical work takes any course (not just critical) and reducing it by any value will cause the «enlightenment and entertainment» activity's duration to reduce by the same value;

b) In shortening a chain of critical tasks, which has several parallel chains of uncritical tasks, one should aim at a minimum sum of free time reserve on a parallel sub-critical chain. If all the free reserves of tasks of a sub-critical chain are used, the latter will take a critical course.

After reducing in the duration of separate tasks lying on a critical course, network parameters are being counted out again since new critical courses may appear. It often happens, that after a reduction of critical tasks, when using up all the reserves of time in sub-critical courses one cannot complete the whole operation within a given time. In this case, one should repeat the operation of reducing critical tasks (taking into account changes in the graph, which occurred after the first reduction), and compute network parameters again. Operations for reducing critical tasks are repeated until a definite time-frame for all the «enlightenment and entertainment» measurement preparations is reached.

Reducing the duration for the completion of individual tasks can be achieved at the expense of attracting extra material and financial resources and labor forces, as well as redistributing resources among participating institutions.

The data obtained from the calculations allows us to make a prognosis of events and determine the further course of the network graph. Such a prognosis allows a reaction in good time to any possible disruption of a completion deadline, resource redistribution, changes in critical course, i.e. to bring such qualitative changes in a network model, which will provide successful completion of the whole complex of «enlightenment and entertainment» measures within set terms.

Operational management tasks among a cultural institutions' activities may be solved by computers. This will allow us to correct a working plan daily, i.e. to know which stage we are at, what kind of work is being left out, which task is behind schedule and how to correct a situation. Taking into account a changing situation, the computers E.C.M will conduct calculations and present a corrected plan of action for the whole «enlightenment and entertainment» personnel of a region for any given moment in time.

D. A PRODUCTION FUNCTION MODEL OF THE «ENLIGHTENMENT AND ENTERTAINMENT BRANCHES»

Creation of an economic mathematical model for the «enlightenment and entertainment branches» production placement and development creates great opportunities for imitating socio-economic processes of «enlightenment and entertainment» activities and a multi-versioned prognosis of development.

When constructing a production function for «enlightenment and entertainment branches» model, one begins with the fact that «enlightenment and entertainment» enterprises appear as systems whose components (fixed assets, labor forces) interact, through certain technologies with a specific subject of labor—an individual—in time and space. As a result, a «enlightenment and entertainment service» is created, which may be measured in units of time and cost.

In a general form, a production function for «enlightenment and entertainment» activities can be written as follows:

$$V = f(x_1, x_2, \ldots x_n),$$

where

$x_1 = (1, 2, \ldots n)$—factors of production;

V—volume of «enlightenment and entertainment service» production on assimilation of the population's spare time resource.

The correlation between the volume of «enlightenment and entertainment service» production (V) and the volume of resources of past (F) and direct (L) labor may be written as follows:

$$V = A_0 \cdot F^\alpha \cdot L^\beta \quad (1)[41]$$

where

a, b—ratios of efficiency of replacement of past and direct labor;

A_0—a scale ratio.

The proposed production function reflects an objective interaction of factors of this special production force with the «enlightenment and entertainment» results.

The main standards required of a production function for «enlightenment and entertainment» activities are as follows:

---

[41] As a basis for this model (1) we take the degree function, as follows:

$$V = a_0 \prod_{i=1}^{n} x_i^{a_i}$$

where V—volume of «enlightenment and entertainment service» production;

xi—a factor of production;

a_0, a_1, a_2, a_n—regression ratios.

a) the variables included in a production function must be quantitatively measurable;

b) in case of limitations on material resources as well as the population's spare time resource, production of this activity cannot grow limitlessly;

c) the resources reflected in a production function are necessary, and the absence of even one of them nullifies the results;

d) the resources functioning in «enlightenment and entertainment» process must be interchangeable to a certain extent;

e) the «enlightenment and entertainment» activity results must be quantitatively measurable;

f) a production's function must be uninterrupted and differentiable.

Since both past and direct labor is used up relatively autonomously in such «enlightenment and entertainment» process, a certain part of the equipment (musical equipment) can create «enlightenment and entertainment service» independently. This allows us to write the following equation:

$$V = \frac{\partial V}{\partial F} \cdot F + \frac{\partial V}{\partial F} \cdot L$$

The essence of this equation is that production of services to assimilate the population's spare time resource is realized at the expense of direct labor, while only a part of STP is realized at the expense of past labor.

A special role in the production of the «enlightenment and entertainment branch» belongs to the «fixed assets armament» criterion, which is written in the form of the relationship (F/L). It reflects an organic structure of the production force of this branch. It may be applied to a separate institution as well. The relationship (dF/dL) may be called a limit norm for replacement of factors in the process of «enlightenment and entertainment service» production.

This relationship can be written as follows:

$$\frac{dF}{dL} : \frac{dL}{L} = \frac{dF}{dL} \cdot \frac{L}{F} = \frac{dF}{dL} : \frac{F}{L} = K$$

K—value that characterizes the changing limit norm of substitution (%).

At the same time, an elasticity ratio on the material conditions of «enlightenment and entertainment» activities can be written as follows:

$$\alpha = \frac{\partial V}{\partial F} \cdot \frac{F}{V}$$

While for labor:

$$\beta = \frac{\partial V}{\partial L} \cdot \frac{L}{V}$$

a and b—elasticity ratios for a volume of «enlightenment and entertainment service» production for both past and direct labor respectively. Each of them shows by what value a volume of assimilated STP resource grows, as one of the limiting resources increase in volume given the constant level of others.

The correlation a/b is called an elastic replacement correlation, meaning that the correlation between past and direct labor changes with the changes to the limit norm replacement factors. Thus, if a limit norm of replacement increases by 1 per cent, that means that the volume of fixed assets will increase by 1 per cent.

One should especially point out the functional relation between criteria of socio-economic efficiency, arrived at by dividing the production function of «enlightenment and entertainment branches» by L:

$$\frac{V}{L} = \gamma \frac{F^{\alpha} \cdot L^{\beta}}{L}, \quad \frac{V}{L} = \gamma \cdot F^{\alpha} \cdot L^{\beta-1}, \text{ or } \frac{V}{L} = \gamma \left(\frac{F}{L} \right)^{\alpha}_{\alpha+\beta=1}$$

We arrive at the dependence of the change of direct labor productivity in the «enlightenment and entertainment branches» on «fixed assets armament».

978-0-595-41959-3
0-595-41959-3

www.ingramcontent.com/pod-product-compliance
Lightning Source LLC
Chambersburg PA
CBHW030932180526
45163CB00002B/536